For Better
Not Worse

Transforming Your Marriage
from a Contract to a Covenant

BY

DR. DAVID C. COOPER

FOR BETTER NOT WORSE!
Transforming Your Marriage From A Contract To A Covenant

ISBN 0-9668382-0-3

This book is dedicated to Barbie, my faithful wife and best friend whose steadfast commitment has shown me the meaning of covenant love.

C O N T E N T S

P A R T   I
BUILDING ON THE RIGHT FOUNDATION

P A R T   I I
PAYING ATTENTION TO THE PIVOTAL POINTS

P A R T   I I I
KEEPING YOUR HOUSE IN ORDER

INTRODUCTION

When Hannibal crossed the Rubican he watched until the last of his troops crossed the river and then he ordered the bridges to be burned. Hence, we have the phrase, "burning bridges behind you." It was his way of assuring that his troops would have no opportunity for retreat. It was a decisive moment of total commitment to a cause that had to succeed — and succeed it did.

Marriage begins with a decisive moment of total commitment based on unconditional love between a man and a woman "till death us do part." Marriage is for life. But today marriages are breaking up at an alarming rate and with an unprecedented intensity.

Did you know that...

- The average marriage in the United States lasts only 9.4 years.
- Every 27 seconds a couple divorces, totaling approximately 7,000 divorces per day, affecting some 10,000 children.
- Divorce rates have doubled since 1965 and demographers project that half of all first marriages will end in divorce as well as 60 percent of all second marriages.[1]
- Marital stress costs Americans $2.9 billion a year in lost work and productivity.[2]

Why do marriages fail? While many reasons could be cited perhaps the main reason is the loss of understanding of marriage as a covenant relationship. We tend to think of marriage more in terms of a ceremony, a custom or a contract than we do a covenant.

After listening to couples pour out their marital frustrations and disappointments in countless counseling sessions, I am convinced that the lack of covenant commitment lies at the heart of most fractured marriages. To put it frankly, couples have contracts instead of covenants.

What's the difference? You may ask. A contract consists of demands and expectations, bargaining and negotiation, an equal give-and-take in a relationship. In other words, you get what you pay for. A contract is a 50/50 proposition. If one party fails to live up to his end of the contract the deal is off. I do my part if you do your part. The problem is, marriage will not work very well as a contract.

A covenant, on the other hand, is a relationship based on unconditional love. Covenant love means being willing to sacrifice your needs for the needs of another. It remains faithful to its commitment, regardless of the cost. Marriage is not a 50/50 agreement; it's a 100 percent commitment of a husband and wife to each other without counting the cost. Expecting nothing in return. No strings attached. While a contract exists as a commercial or litigious binding of two parties, the covenant constitutes a relationship characterized by unconditional love which cannot be broken.

Covenant love affects every aspect of a marriage from communication skills to making decisions, from money-management to raising children and from spirituality to sexual intimacy. When a couple builds their marriage on covenant love they spend their lives trying to out-give each other. And they end up getting more than they ever imagined possible.

If there is one message I want to stress throughout this book, it is the assurance that marriage can be the most wonderful, rewarding and fulfilling experience in this life. You don't have to buy into the negative press about marriage perpetuated today. There are too many people who take Plato's humorous assessment of marriage seriously:

"One ought to marry at all costs, for if it proves to be a happy relationship, one will experience bliss and heavenly delight. If it proves to be an unhappy relationship, one may then become a philosopher and experience the joys of the mind."

Let me assure you, you don't have to give up marriage and become a philosopher to be happy. You can be happy and married — *for better not worse!* The key lies in having a covenant, not a contract.

Sound intriguing?

Believe me, it is.

Read on and let's see how it's done.

CHAPTER ONE

SEVEN MYTHS OF MARRIAGE

T HE SPACE SHUTTLE *DISCOVERY* WAS GROUNDED RECENTLY—NOT BY technical difficulties or the lack of government funding, but by woodpeckers. Yellow-shafted flicker woodpeckers found the insulating foam on the shuttle's fuel tank irresistible material for pecking. The foam is crucial to the shuttle's performance. Without it, ice forms on the tank when it is filled with the super-cold fuel, ice that can break free during liftoff and damage the spacecraft. The shuttle was grounded until the damage could be repaired.

False ideas or myths about marriage are like woodpeckers that peck away at a relationship. Such myths tend to make us prone to unhealthy demands and to possess unrealistic expectations of marriage. When what we want out of marriage is not what we get, we become dissatisfied. Regardless of how hard we try, we can't make the relationship exactly the way we want it. The end result is often divorce due to "irreconcilable differences." Simply translated, we grow tired of each other, get bored with the relationship and want out. That about sums it up for a lot of couples today.

What is your mental picture of marriage? How do you see it?

Some people envision having the perfect marriage. After a few years, however, when they realize their marriage will never be perfect, they decide they married the wrong person. Let's be perfectly honest, no couple has a perfect marriage. I once read that Adam and Eve were the only couple who had a perfect marriage. He didn't have to hear about all the men she could have married, and she didn't have to hear about his mother's cooking. Well, excluding Adam and Eve, the rest of us have to deal with imperfect marriages.

On top of that, because of secular influences which often take a dim view of marriage, along with a high divorce rate that makes many people leery of marriage, the institution of marriage is getting a bad rap today. Some people can identify with the man who said, "Marriage may be a divine institution, but I'm not ready for an institution yet."

So, what does it take to have a happy marriage? I once read that a happy marriage is when a couple is as deeply in love as they are in debt. In reality, couples are happily married when they share a covenant together instead of a contract. This means we need to dispel the myths of marriage that keep us from covenant living.

I've identified seven myths in particular that we need to lay to rest for good.

MYTH #1: MARRIAGE IS AN EVENT

A wedding is an event but marriage is a process. Today the average age of couples getting married is 24.1 years for brides and 26.3 years for grooms while the average cost of a wedding is $16,000. The average cost of an engagement ring is $3,000. Sales of engagement and wedding rings amount to $3.3 billion a year.[1]

As you know, a wedding takes months to prepare. Selecting the dresses and tuxedos for the wedding party, choosing the music, arranging the florist, preparing the rehearsal dinner and the wedding reception, selecting the wedding invitations, and the list goes on and on.

Finally, the big day arrives. I can't count the times I've stood with an anxious groom waiting for the wedding service to begin who asks me, "Pastor, how long will the service last?" I usually respond, "Not nearly as long as the marriage." Unfortunately, we get the two confused.

In the Book of Genesis we find the best definition of marriage ever given: *"For this reason a man will leave his father and mother and be united to his wife, and they will become one flesh."*[2] While the verse is rich with meaning, I want you to think about the passive verb *become.* It speaks of the process of growth and development. Marriage is a process — not an event!

The wedding service itself does not instantaneously fuse a husband and wife together as one. Achieving oneness takes time — a lifetime, in fact. Gradually, through the seasons of married life a couple grows together through the ups and downs, the joys and sorrows, the triumphs and tragedies to become one flesh. Webster says that growth means to increase in size, amount and degree; to come to be gradually; and to progress toward maturity. As C.S. Lewis remarked, "You can't stay a good egg forever." Marriages either grow or die, develop or deteriorate, progress or regress.

Perfectionism is a big problem for many couples today. The perfectionist demands everything to be right, all the time, with no room for failure. It's all or nothing with a perfectionist because he or she doesn't understand growth. Couples caught in the trap of striving for a perfect marriage are doomed for failure and frustration.

Remember, your marriage is only what you make it today. What happened yesterday, good or bad, doesn't determine the quality of your relationship. You determine its quality by the way you treat each other through every little action of the common day. The past is gone. Tomorrow is yet to come. Today is all you have. *Carpe deum—* Seize the day!

Unfortunately, many couples lack the vision they need to take their marriage to a new level. Solomon reminds us, *"Where there is no vision the people perish."* So it is with marriage—without a vision couples perish. Here are some of the worst predictions ever made that illustrate the problem of limited vision:

- "Everything that can be invented has been invented."
  U.S. PATENT OFFICE DIRECTOR URGING PRESIDENT MCKINLEY TO ABOLISH THE OFFICE IN 1899
- "I think there is a world market for about five computers."
  THOMAS J. WATSON, IBM IN 1958
- "Any general system of conveying passengers at a velocity exceeding 10 miles per hour is extremely improbable."
  THOMAS TREGOLD, BRITISH RAILROAD DESIGNER, 1835
- "The population of the earth decreases every day. In another 10 centuries the earth will be nothing but a desert."
  MONTESQUIEU, 1743
- "While theoretically and technically television may be feasible, commercially and financially I consider it an impossibility, a development of which we need waste little time dreaming." LEE DEFOREST, AMERICAN INVENTOR, 1926
- "I cannot conceive of anything more ridiculous, more absurd and more affrontive to sober judgment than the cry that we are profiting by the acquisition of California and New Mexico. I hold that they are not worth a dollar."
  SENATOR DANIEL WEBSTER, 1848
- "So many centuries after the Creation it is unlikely that anyone could find at this point unknown lands of any value." IN A REPORT GIVEN TO KING FERDINAND AND QUEEN ISABELLA OF SPAIN IN 1486[3]

Talk about a lack of vision! Where would the world be today had we listened to these negativists? We would still be in the dark ages.

Now, let me ask you, What kind of vision do your have for your marriage? Remember the adage, "If you aim at nothing you will probably hit it." Happy marriages are grown slowly over the years by couples who possess a sense of where they're going and how they plan to get there.

One day a passerby observed the construction of a magnificent cathedral. As he passed a group of brick masons working on the project he asked one of them, "What are you doing?"

He replied, "I'm laying brick."

He asked another worker, "What are you doing?"

"I'm constructing a wall," the man replied.

Finally, he asked a third mason, "What are you building?"

He responded enthusiastically, "I'm erecting a cathedral!"

What kind of marriage are you building? Are you just laying bricks or building walls—going through the daily routines of married life without any rhyme or reason? Or, are you building a great cathedral?

MYTH #2: MY MATE WILL CHANGE AFTER WE GET MARRIED

This myth causes couples to enter marriage with hidden agendas which foster unrealistic expectations and demands. The antidote to such hidden agendas is: *acceptance* and *respect*. What a difference it would make in our homes if we lived by Romans 15:7, *"Accept one another, then, just as Christ accepted you."* And how does Christ accept us? He accepts us just like we are—unconditionally!

As a small boy I remember when the first Burger King opened in our neighborhood. What I liked best about Burger King was their slogan: "Come as you are." Of course, my mother never would let us do that. She always made us clean up and dress up. Nonetheless, I liked the idea of going out to eat wearing my play clothes and not having to change.

That's acceptance—come as you are. Happily married couples accept each other unconditionally. They even accept things they don't like about each other. They focus on their similarities rather than their differences.

They also respect each other. Respect means to highly regard and esteem another person. The root of the word *respect* means "to look at"—that is to behold the true beauty of another person with an eye of discerning love. Francine Klagsbrum interviewed 87 couples who were married for 15 years or longer to identify the factors that enabled their marriages to thrive. The key ingredient she found was respect.[4]

Psychologist Carl Rogers said, "When I walk on the beach to watch the sunset I do not look up at the sky and demand, 'How about a little more orange over to the right please,' or 'Would you mind putting a little less purple in the background?' No, I enjoy the always different sunsets as they are. We would do well to do the same with the people we love."

MYTH #3: MY MATE WON'T CHANGE AFTER WE GET MARRIED

Change is fundamental to life. Every living organism on the planet undergoes the processes of change and development. Only inanimate objects never change. While change can be stressful to a marriage, because it disrupts the status quo, it also brings positive and rewarding results. One way to measure your stress points is to add up the changes you face in life, like having a new baby, buying a new home, or receiving a job promotion. Not only do outward circumstances change, people change. When they do, their relationships are forced to change as well. So, happily married couples handle change well.

During counseling sessions, I've often heard a dissatisfied husband complain about his wife, "She's not the person I married 15 years ago." Or a wife remark, "He's not the man I married 20 years ago." When I hear those kinds of statements I immediately respond, "Whatever gave you the idea he or she would stay the same throughout your marriage?" After all, who stays the same for 15 or 20 years?

Married or not, people continue to change throughout the course of their lives. Well, you may be asking right now, What changes usually occur in a marriage? It would be easier to answer, What doesn't change? In reality, everything is subject to change. Personalities. Interests. Hobbies. Educations. Careers. Personal goals. You name it, and it can change.

Certainly one's physical appearance changes over the years. Today, at least, we have a variety of products to help us counteract these changes and maintain a more youthful look—make-up, cosmetic surgery, hair replacement and so forth. In spite of these helps, we still face the reality of aging bodies.

I heard about a man who went shopping with his wife for some new dress slacks. She noticed that he had put on several pounds around the waist and remarked, "It's amazing when you realize it takes an oak tree 200 years to get that big around!"

I'll tell you something else that changes — ladies' hairstyles. And sometimes daily. In fact for husbands who are newlyweds, let me share with you some invaluable wisdom at this point which every husband who has been married for any length of time has learned the hard way. When your wife asks you how you like her new hair style, don't answer. Take the Fifth Amendment. It's a no-win situation. If you say, "I liked it better the old way," she'll say you don't love her. And if you say, "It looks great," she'll accuse you of lying.

I heard about one lady who set her hair with some new high-tech rollers. When her husband got home, he took one look at all the paraphernalia in her hair and blurted out, "Good heavens—what did you do to your hair?"

She said, "I just set it."

He snapped back, "Well, when's it gonna go off?"

The point is—things change. Happily married couples adapt to the changes that take place through the seasons of married life — the engagement, the honeymoon, the early years, the child-rearing years, the empty nest, and, finally, retirement. They make what one psychologist calls "strategic midcourse corrections." Couples who stay together in the face of significant changes do so because they go through periodic seasons of remarriage. They continue to choose each other as partners for life.

MYTH #4: MARRIAGE IS HARD WORK

While it certainly is true that marriage can be hard work, and is for a number of couples, it doesn't have to be. This myth is perpetuated by those who are down on marriage. Also, the high divorce rate has left many people leery of marriage. For some, being happily married for life seems like the impossible dream.

The attack against the traditional family is seen in the growing trend of some women deliberately choosing to raise children without the father. Katha Pollitt asks, "Why not have a child on one's own? Children are a joy; many men are not." Actress Michelle Pfeiffer adds, in justifying her decision to raise a child on her own, "Men are like pinch hitters. So what's the deal?" [5]

You may remember when, in 1992, then Vice President Dan Quayle criticized the *CBS* sitcom *Murphy Brown* for its episode heralding the virtue of an out-of-wedlock birth by the heroine Brown. Quayle was not suggesting that every woman who has a child out-of-wedlock is a scourge on society. He was simply criticizing the new notion that suggests fathers are no longer necessary in the process of raising children. It is interesting that the next year Barbara Defore

Whitehead published an article in *The Atlantic Monthly* entitled, "Dan Quayle Was Right."

However, if marriage is going to be a joy and not a burden, two pitfalls need to be avoided. The first is *negligence.* When couples neglect the garden of love, the weeds of resentment, stagnation and friction grow up destroying their relationship. Love does not grow on its own; it must be nurtured carefully. Marriage will not fly on auto-pilot; couples must keep their hands on the controls and guide its course to insure a safe flight.

The second pitfall to avoid is *sabotage.* Some people sabotage the joyful marriage they could have through such destructive behaviors as affairs, abuse, alcoholism, drug abuse and abandonment. Also, the lesser sins of constant criticism, uncontrolled anger and deep-seated resentments eat away at a marriage until, eventually, nothing is left.

If you avoid these two pitfalls—negligence and sabotage—marriage is not hard work; it's a relationship of unspeakable joy and fulfillment.

Myth #5: My Mate Can, Will And Should Meet All My Needs

What a detrimental myth. Such thinking stifles a marriage with smothering demands and unrealistic expectations. To be sure, we all have needs; and, marriage does help meet many of them. But it is pure fantasy to think that one's partner can meet every need.

Everyone has three basic needs: *the need for significance*—to possess self-esteem, self-awareness and a positive self-image; *the need for inclusion*—to be part of a group larger than ourselves such as family, friends, work or church; and *the need for contribution*—to make a productive contribution to others during the course of one's lifetime.

Beyond these basic needs men and women have some important

needs that are met through marriage. Willard F. Harley identifies the top five needs of husbands and wives in his book, *His Needs, Her Needs*. According to his research, the top five needs of husbands are: sexual fulfillment, recreational companionship, an attractive wife, domestic support, and admiration. The top five needs of wives are: affection, conversation, honesty and openness, financial support and family commitment.[6]

While marriage certainly meets many of these needs, it doesn't meet them all. Such an unrealistic expectation of marriage only results in disappointment. Overly needy people drain the life and love out of their marriage leaving it an empty well.

Instead of depending so heavily on your partner, try drawing on your relationship to God. Only He can meet your needs. This is what the apostle Paul meant when he said, *"I can do everything through him who gives me strength."* Then added, *"My God will meet all your needs according to his glorious riches in Christ Jesus."*[7] What a fantastic promise! Only when we depend on God to meet our needs are we free to relate to others without forming co-dependent relationships.

Also, people need to develop a sense of individual freedom and identity. You've probably said on one occasion, "I need my space." I know it sounds like a cliché out of the seventies, but it's true—we all need our space. Autonomy. Individuality. Freedom.

There are two types of unhealthy marriages. The first is the *detached marriage*, in which a husband and wife live together like strangers who pass in the night. The only thing they share in common is the house or apartment where they live.

On the other hand, the *enmeshed marriage* consists of a couple whose lives are so intertwined that neither one possesses individuality. I observed this type of relationship on one particular occasion while counseling an engaged couple. The young man did most of the talking and prefaced nearly every statement with the pronoun "we." "We feel like..." or "We're frustrated with...." He kept saying "we" when he actually meant "I." So, I encouraged him to change his "we" statements to "I" statements. This helped him express his own thoughts and feelings and not to speak for his wife to be. This gave her the freedom to speak for herself.

Happily married couples strike a balance between independence and dependence, achieving a state of *interdependence.* The interdependent couple knows when to stand apart in individuality and when to come together in unity. They know which needs can be met through the marriage as well as those that can be met through other relationships and activities.

All marriages have limitations. Underscore the word *all.* Nobody's marriage is going to give them everything they want, or even need no matter how much they ask for it, demand it or even pray for it. Until a couple learns to accept the limitations of their marriage they will never experience the joy of contentment.

Today, marriages are deeply troubled by discontentment. When discontentment sets in, couples grow restless at home and fantasize about what life would be like with another person who they imagine (falsely, I might add) can meet all their needs. Fantasy thinking gets people in deep trouble, generating feelings of discontentment, ingratitude and anger. It sets couples on a collision course with disaster.

Contentment is vital to happiness. So, accept the limitations of your marriage and make the most with what you have. Gratefully receive the love your partner gives emotionally, spiritually and romantically. And resist the temptation to expect more than is realistic. As the Bible says, "In *everything give thanks for this is the will of God in Christ Jesus concerning you.*"[8] That's sound advice for every couple.

MYTH #6: I INTUITIVELY KNOW ALL I NEED TO KNOW ABOUT LOVE AND MARRIAGE

This myth seems to be more prevalent among men than it is among women. Women, by and large, demonstrate a greater interest in learning about marriage and relationships through reading, attending marriage enrichment seminars and going to counseling. There is something in the male ego that prides itself on being self-sufficient.

The fact is no one knows everything he or she needs to know about love and marriage. Everyone has room to grow and much to learn. No couple matures to the place where they have nothing new to learn about each other or about their relationship. This know-it-all attitude only produces stagnation and apathy in marriage.

Let's face it: men and women are fundamentally different. Even Sigmund Freud confessed, "The great question I have not been able to answer is, what does a woman want?" Men struggle to understand women, and women struggle to understand men. Unfortunately, secularism has downplayed our differences by advocating a unisex, genderless society. But no amount of re-education will change the fact that men and women were, are and always will be fundamentally different. Which, by the way, is God's wonderful plan.

While men and women are different, maybe even from different planets, we need to avoid stereotypes. All men are not the same, neither are all women. Which means, that learning what women in general want or need out of marriage is not nearly as important as knowing specifically what your wife wants and needs. In the same way, a wife needs to get in touch with what her husband needs not just learn about what men in general need in marriage.

Couples need to talk together about what each one really needs out of the marriage. Operating on stereotypes can lead to misunderstandings. And remember, by the way, that it takes a lifetime to fully know another person. So enjoy the journey together. Discover your partner's uniqueness and avoid stereotypes.

MYTH #7: ALL YOU NEED IS LOVE

In the sixties, The Beatles sang, "All You Need Is Love." In the seventies, Burt Bacharach sang, "What The World Needs Now Is Love Sweet Love." In the eighties, Tina Turner sang, "What's Love Got To Do With It?" And in the nineties, Michael Bolton sang, "Said I Love You But I Lied." How times change.

The question is, What is love? The myth that says all you need is love defines love as a feeling of romance and infatuation. To be sure, the emotional, romantic aspect of love is a wonderful and vital part of marriage. No marriage is complete without it. Falling in love is the greatest euphoria in the world. But there's more to love than that. Love is a way of acting, not just feeling. Covenant love is measured by the unreserved, unconditional surrender of oneself to another in a steadfast commitment, till death us do part.

My wife, Barbie, taught me an invaluable lesson about covenant love on our wedding day. Since I wrote the wedding ceremony, I was familiar with the order of service. That is until she threw me a curve. After we shared our vows and exchanged rings, the minister paused. Barbie then began to repeat the words spoken by Ruth to Naomi recorded in the Bible. I was caught off guard, to say the least.

> *Don't urge me to leave you or to turn back from you. Where you go I will go, and where you stay I will stay. Your people will be my people and your God my God. Where you die I will die, and there I will be buried. May the Lord deal with me, be it ever so severely, if anything but death separates you and me.* [9]

Although I retained my composure publicly, I was deeply moved. And I knew she meant what she was saying. Her words to me that day embodied the essence of covenant love. A love that transcends feelings and functions as an act of the will; a love that treats others with the same compassion, understanding, tenderness, forgiveness and grace with which God treats us.

Max Lucado offers a beautiful wedding prayer that touches on the constancy of covenant love.

Create in us a love, O Lord.

An eternal love...Your love.

A love that forgives any failure,

spans any distance,

withstands any tempest.

Create in us a love, O Lord.

A new love.

A fresh love.

A love with the tenderness of a lamb,

the grandeur of a mountain,

the strength of a lion.

And make us one. Intimately one.

As you made a hundred colors into one sunset,

A thousand cedars into one forest,

and countless stars into one galaxy . . .

make our two hearts as one, Father, forever...

that you may be praised, Father, forever.[10]

IT'S ALL ABOUT TRUST

Love means trust. If a husband and wife don't trust each other, they won't make it together very long. Let me share with you how Barbie and I learned the importance of trust in our marriage. She and I come from entirely different family backgrounds. I grew up in a stable, Christian home, sort of the all-American family. She, on the other hand, grew up in what we sometimes call a dysfunctional family. By the time she graduated from high school, the family had nearly completely disintegrated due to alcoholism and destructive relational patterns.

I remember an incident during our first year of marriage when we had a disagreement. She reacted in a way that totally caught me off guard. In a moment of frustration she said, "Maybe we made a mistake by getting married."

At first I passed it off as nothing, until another time when she reacted to an argument by blurting out, "Maybe we should just get a divorce."

"A divorce?" I thought to myself. "What in the world is she talking about?"

We quickly made up and she forgot she said it. She never really meant to say such a thing in the first place. She merely spoke out of her frustration and anger.

I prayed for several days asking the Lord to give me insight into what she was feeling. Then, one day, I sat down with her on the couch and said, "Honey, let me share something with you. It has occurred to me that when I stood at the altar of the church and shared my vows to love you till death us do part, that you really don't believe I meant what I said. I also realize that the reason you don't trust me when I say 'I love you,' is largely due to the fact that, when the most important people in your life, your parents, told you they loved you, they let you down. From now on, I want you to know that I meant what I said at the altar. Regardless of what we may face together or whatever disagreements we may have, nothing will ever change the commitment I made to you when we shared our wedding vows. When we talk about an issue, we are doing just that, talking about an *issue*. We are not reevaluating the covenant we made together. Our covenant is secure. And over the years, you will learn to trust my love for you."

As I said, that has been nearly nineteen years ago. I can assure you she no longer struggles with whether or not I love her. She knows beyond a shadow of a doubt that there is nothing that can separate her from my love. She has learned that there are some people in this world who mean it when they say it—"I love you."

I want to add something here that may be of tremendous benefit, especially for younger couples. After that conversation, we set a rule that the word *divorce* would never again be spoken in our home — and it never has. I am suggesting this because couples sometimes throw the word around when they get angry and frustrated. The more the word divorce is used as a threat the more it becomes a viable option. So avoid it. Use your energies more productively—to build a strong, stable marriage for the glory of God.

Covenant love goes beyond any contract a couple can devise. In a contract when one party fails to fulfill the terms, meet the conditions or satisfy the agreement, the deal is off. But covenant love is like the Energizer Bunny—in spite of disappointments, failures and sins, it keeps going and going and going...till death us do part.

THE MYTH SAYS... THE TRUTH IS...

Let's recap the seven myths of marriage:

- *The myth says, Marriage is an event.* The truth is marriage is a life-long journey together; a gradual and joyful process of development in which two people become one flesh.

- *The myth says, My mate will change after we are married.* The truth is covenant love means to love another person unconditionally, with acceptance and respect for their uniqueness.

- *The myth says, My mate will not change after we are married.* The truth is we all continue to grow and change throughout the seasons of life. Happily married couples learn to joyfully accept those changes and make appropriate adjustments.

- *The myth says, Marriage is hard work.* The truth is marriage is a joyful experience unless a couple neglects each other or sabotages their relationship through destructive behavior like abuse, drugs, affairs or abandonment.

- *The myth says, My mate can, will and should meet all my needs.* The truth is we need to depend on God to meet our needs. Couples also need to strive for interdependence in marriage—the delicate balance of dependence and independence.

- *The myth says, I intuitively know all I need to know about love and marriage.* The truth is, everyone has much to learn about their partner and this thing called marriage.

- *The myth says, All you need is love.* The truth is love is more than a romantic feeling; covenant love is strong and steadfast, remaining true to its vows regardless of the cost.

Now that we've laid these myths to rest, we're ready to explore the wonderful world of covenant love.

CHAPTER TWO

COVENANT VERSUS CONTRACT

T HE MODERN DAY CONTRACTUAL APPROACH TO MARRIAGE HAS FAILED miserably. As James Q. Wilson of the University of California, Los Angeles writes:

The contemporary legal system views people as autonomous individuals endowed with rights and entering into real or implied contracts. The liberalization of law pertaining to marriage and divorce arose out of just such a view. Marriage, once a sacrament, has become in the eyes of the law a contract that is easily negotiated, renegotiated, or rescinded. Within a few years, no-fault divorce on demand became possible, after millennia in which such an idea would have been unthinkable. It is now easier to renounce a marriage than a mortgage; at least the former occurs much more frequently than the latter.[1]

A recent newspaper headline caught my attention: "TENNESSEE CONSIDERING 'COVENANT MARRIAGE' LEGISLATION." In an attempt to strengthen marriages and cut down on divorces, Tennessee legislators are considering a "covenant marriage" bill. Louisiana has already adopted such a measure. The Louisiana bill allows couples to obtain a marriage covenant instead of a traditional marriage license. Couples sign a declaration in which they agree that marriage is a commitment to live together for life, they have chosen each other carefully and disclosed to each other "everything which could adversely affect" their marriage.[2]

They must also complete required premarital counseling and agree that if they experience difficulty they will commit themselves to trying to preserve their marriage. The counseling, which is paid for by the couple, must be conducted by a member of the clergy or a licensed counselor.

Couples who choose a covenant marriage license may get divorced only after receiving counseling and only for a specified list of reasons including adultery, commission of a felon, abandonment for at least one year, separation for at least two years, or the physical or sexual abuse of a spouse or a child of either spouse. The goal of the legislature is not to make divorce more difficult but to make marriages more successful.

That's encouraging news. Now, even states are seeking measures to strengthen marriages. Why? Because there's a national epidemic of divorces and fractured families. And the main cause is the breakdown of marriage as a covenant relationship.

Let me ask you, How do you define marriage? Is it a covenant or a contract?

I suppose everyone has some kind of a definition. One person said, "Marriage is like a three ring circus. First, you have the engagement ring, then wedding ring, and finally, the suffering."

Someone else observed that, "Marriage is an adventure. It's like going off to war."

Here's a favorite of mine: "Marriage is like a midnight phone call — you get a ring and then you wake up!"

The Bible says that marriage becomes a reality when a man leaves his father and mother and cleaves to his wife so that they become one flesh. You have to leave before you can cleave. Some couples have a hard time "cleaving" because they never really leave home. It's like the young girl who went to talk to her father one night about getting married.

"Dad, Tom has asked me to marry him," she said excitedly.

"That's great sweetheart."

"Yes, but I don't know what I should do," she said.

Her father replied, "What do you mean you don't know what to do? Don't you want to marry Tom?"

"Oh, yes," she said, "but I can't stand the thought of leaving mother."

"Well, don't let that stop you," he said, "take your mother with you!"

WHAT IS A COVENANT?

Marriage is a covenant relationship based on unconditional love and steadfast commitment till death us do part. But, you may ask, What is a covenant? Since the concept of a covenant is so deeply rooted in the Bible we need to begin here in our search for a definition. The concept of marriage as a covenant is based on the concept of God's relationship with His people. That's why in the Old Testament Israel is referred to as the bride or wife of Jehovah.[3] Again, in the New Testament, the Church is called the bride of Christ and is portrayed as *"a bride beautifully dressed for her husband."*[4]

Paul the Apostle concludes his celebrated passage on marriage by writing, *"This is a profound mystery but I am talking about Christ and the Church."*[5] The provocative interplay between God's covenant love for His people and the relationship of a husband and wife provides a clear picture of the marriage covenant.

A covenant is essentially a "compact or agreement between two parties binding them mutually to undertakings on each other's behalf."[6] Furthermore, it can be seen as "a solemn promise made binding by an oath, which may be either a verbal formula or a symbolic action. Such an action or formula is recognized by both parties as the formal act which binds the actor to fulfill his promise."[7] Arnold Rhodes says that a covenant is "a binding of persons in a special relationship."[8]

As important as these definitions are, however, they fail to make the distinction between a covenant and a contract—a distinction which is crucial to make. Now follow me closely. While a covenant and a contract appear to be the same, they are in fact, polar opposites. That means, what is true of a covenant is not true of a contract and vice versa. In fact, the word translated covenant in the Bible is never used to describe a mutual treaty or a contract.

Listen carefully to how one scholar explains this important truth: "The Greek understanding of the term *diatheke* (covenant) suggests that the covenant was no longer an agreement between two parties with equal rights. It came about as an exclusively divine action, which men can only accept in the form in which it is given to them."[9]

A covenant *does not* consist of a negotiated agreement between two parties, as in the case of a contract. Nowhere in the Bible does covenant mean "mutual treaty."[10] A covenant, then, must be understood as a one-party agreement which the other party may accept or reject, but not alter or negate.

Think about God's covenant of love with us in Christ Jesus. God took the sole initiative in establishing the covenant simply because He loves us. We played no part in the making of the covenant. Who among us has ascended into heaven to speak with God face to face and negotiate the terms, conditions and benefits of God's plan of salvation? God and God alone established the terms, met the conditions and provided the benefits of the covenant for us. It was all His doing. Our role is one of response: to either accept or reject His covenant of salvation in Jesus Christ. As John the Apostle said, *"Yet to all who received him, to those who believed in his name, he gave the right to become children of God."*[11]

This is seen clearly in the terminology God uses when He makes a covenant. The key phrase in all biblical covenants is, *I will.* When God declares *I will,* He is saying, "I am taking the initiative to make and keep the covenant with you purely because I love you and desire a relationship with you." When you read such passages you will notice something missing — the condition, "You will." God doesn't say, "I will do this if you will do that." Such terminology would be characteristic of a contract. He simply declares His intention to act on our behalf because He loves us.[12]

So it is with marriage. A husband and wife give unconditionally their love to each other in a covenant as opposed to negotiating a contract. This feature, more than anything else, distinguishes a covenant from a contract.

Now we have a definition: *The marriage covenant is an agreement or promise made by one party to another, on the basis of unconditional love, which the other party may either accept or reject but may not alter or negate.*

Let's build on this foundation as we broaden our understanding of the marriage covenant.

COVENANT LOVE

What do we mean by the term "covenant love?" and what makes covenant love so unique and special? Love is the ageless theme of poets and philosophers, artists and musicians, sculptors and writers. Unfortunately, while we hail love as the greatest of all virtues, true love seems to be glaringly absent from many marriages and homes.

The Hebrew word for covenant love is *hesed.* It appears 240 times in the Old Testament and means loving kindness, loyal love, steadfast love, grace, mercy, faithfulness, goodness and devotion. The word is so rich in its meaning that it takes three words woven tightly together to really define it: *strength, steadfastness,* and *love.*[13] Love, when left alone, can easily become sentimentalized. Strength and steadfastness round out the meaning of love putting some teeth into it. Covenant love remains strong and steadfast through the spiritual, financial and relational storms every married couple face.

When I think about God's *hesed* I'm reminded of a cartoon comic strip of Dennis the Menace. In the cartoon Dennis and his friend Joey leave Mrs. Wilson's house with their hands full of cookies. Joey says to Dennis, "I wonder what we did to deserve this?" Dennis responds, "Look, Joey, Mrs. Wilson gives us cookies not because we're nice but because she's nice." So it is with God. He loves us because of who He is not because of who we are or what we do.

Let's go one step further. The Hebrew word *hesed* corresponds to the New Testament Greek word *agape.* The ancient Greeks used four different words for love: *phileo,* meaning brotherly love; *storge,* meaning family love; *eros,* meaning sexual love; and *agape,* meaning divine love. While the word *agape* was seldom used in classical Greek literature. The New Testament writers picked up the word and filled their writings with it. *Agape* is the love of God. They had seen *agape* in Jesus Christ. He is love incarnate. *Agape* moves from the abstract to the concrete in Christ. He is covenant love in action. Covenant love in marriage, then, means that a husband and wife love each other as Christ loves them.

And how does Christ love us? His love is *selfless*, for He prayed, "Not my will but yours be done." His love is *sacrificial*, for He declared, "Greater love has no man than this, that a man lay down his life for his friends." His love *serves*, for He said, "The Son of man did not come to be served, but to serve, and to give His life a ransom for many."

He doesn't love us *if...*

He doesn't love us *because of...*

He loves us *in spite of...* our sins, our imperfections and our faults.

Now, when we put the Hebrew *hesed* together with the Greek *agape* the portrait of covenant love comes into focus—a husband and his wife faithfully devoted to each other with unconditional love expressing themself through selflessness, sacrifice and service. The Apostle Paul expresses it best:

Love is patient, love is kind.

Love does not envy, it does not boast, it is not proud.

It is not rude, it is not self-seeking,

  it is not easily angered, it keeps no record of wrongs.

Love does not delight in evil but rejoices with the truth.

Love always protects, always trusts, always hopes, always

  perseveres.

Love never fails.

Herein lies the essence of covenant love—freely and unconditionally giving yourself to your partner—

  for better or worse,

    for richer or poorer,

      in sickness and in health,

        to love and to cherish,

          till death us do part.

EQUALITY OR MUTUALITY?

Let's be honest: Most marriages today resemble more of a contract than they do a covenant. Contracts involve demands and expectations, bargaining and negotiation. A contract is a 50/50 proposition based on an equal give-and-take in the relationship. *Equality* is the word. When marriage functions as a contract, the husband fulfills his role and responsibilities if his wife does the same and vice versa.

As a result couples find themselves making such statements as, "I'll meet you half way," "I'll give in if you'll give in," or "I'll change if you'll change." The key word is *if.* Commitment is always conditional – in a contract.

The problem is, marriage will not work very well as a contract. Marriage works best as a covenant. Relationships requiring an equal give-and-take between both parties often results in disappointment due to unfulfilled expectations, selfishness characterized by seeking the fulfillment of personal needs and manipulative behavior aimed at getting what we want without regard for the needs of the other.

Contracts invariably break down. Someone fails to live up to his or her end of the agreement. Since both a husband and a wife bring unique qualities into their marriage, an equal contribution of resources is unrealistic. They need not expect a 50/50 contribution because neither of them brings to the relationship exactly what the other brings.

Early in my ministry I counseled with a couple for thirteen months. They had both been married and divorced before their current marriage of fourteen years. Their relationship had long since deteriorated into a state of mutual toleration for financial and social reasons. A seemingly insurmountable wall of resentment, bitterness and unforgiveness had been built up between them. I wondered if their "Berlin Wall" would ever fall.

Month after month we talked about the need to forgive. But while they agreed that forgiveness was God's command, they seemed incapable of forgiving each other. Their conversations would invariably end with one of them saying to the other, "I'll change what you want me to change *if* you change first." The problem was neither of them was willing to take the first step. You can see their dilemma. Since each one conditioned his actions on the responses of the other, no progress could be made. Someone had to be willing to take the first step. Unfortunately, neither would. Their relationship had reached a stalemate.

I wish I could report that they finally learned how to forgive—that one of them ended the standoff by taking the first step—but they didn't. Eventually, they got divorced. Why? While several issues contributed to their demise, at the bottom of the well was their inability to make the marriage work as a contract. They just couldn't strike the perfect deal where each one got exactly what he or she wanted. One of them had to be willing to lose, to give up their rights, to make the initial sacrifice; but neither of them were. You see, losing isn't an option in a contract.

Only in the covenant can we lose our rights and still experience happiness. In a covenant the goal of marriage is not to have every need or expectation met; the ultimate goal is to give ourselves freely and unconditionally to each other as partners for life.

The most often quoted statement of Jesus recorded in the Gospels underscores this truth: *"Whoever saves his life will lose it, but whoever loses his life for me will find it."* The principle applies to couples as well. The happiest couples are those who are engaged in an endless pursuit of trying to out-give each other.

A BALANCING ACT

Since both a husband and a wife are unique individuals, they don't bring the identical resources into their relationship. The healthy marriage involves a balancing act of a couple's strengths and weaknesses which results in a wealth of shared resources. One partner may actually be a better communicator or a better money-manager or even be more spiritual than the other. That's normal. Opposites do attract (not attack) and can learn a lot from each other. The beauty of marriage is to minimize each other's weaknesses and maximize each other's strengths in the process of learning and living together.

I can honestly say that I am a more complete person, possessing better life-skills and personal qualities as a result of being married to my wife. Now on many points, she and I are polar opposites. These differences were glaringly obvious when we first got married. She was highly organized and I was loose as a goose. She liked to plan every activity (especially vacations), while I liked to play it by ear. Her idea of a vacation involved getting every possible road map, calling the Chamber of Commerce in every city we planned to visit for information on hotels, restaurants and amusements, and planning every minute detail of every day. But my idea of a vacation was to get in the car and say, "Where do you want to go?" We'll plan it as we go along.

I like to improvise—to leave a few things to chance. I guess most men share that trait in common. Men are explorers by nature. This is why men are less likely than women to stop and ask for directions when they're lost. They'd rather find the way on their own. I once heard the question posed: "Why did Moses and the Israelites wander for 40 years in the desert?" Answer: "Because even back then men wouldn't stop to ask for directions!"

Over the years together we've learned to balance each other out: She's less structured and I'm more organized. Our marriage has actually made us both more complete individually as we've acquired new traits from each other. That's what becoming one flesh means.

THE GOLDEN RULE

You may be asking, How do you put covenant love into practice? Jesus tells us how in no uncertain terms: *"Do to others as you would have them do to you."* We call it the Golden Rule. It spells out the meaning of covenant love.

The Golden Rule appears in negative forms in rabbinical Judaism, Hinduism, Buddhism and Confucianism. It also appears in various forms in Greek and Roman ethical teachings. The Golden Rule is a restatement of the Old Testament command: *"Love your neighbor as yourself."* John Locke observed that the Golden Rule lies at the heart of any society as "the most unshakable rule of morality and foundation of social virtue."[14]

Here's the catch—we must interpret the Rule correctly. I have a book of children's letters to God. Whenever I need a good laugh I take it out and read some of their prayers. One little girl named Darla offered the following prayer: "Dear God: Did you really mean do unto others as they do unto you, because if you did then I'm going to fix my brother." Obviously, she misinterpreted the Rule.

Whenever I think about the Golden Rule I can't help but remember when my son David Paul treated his little sister rudely in the car one day. So I told him when he got home to go to his room and write out Luke 6:31 ten times and then we would talk about what it meant. (I don't normally prescribe the Bible for discipline, but I wanted him to think through the implications of the Golden Rule in his own relationships.)

When we got home he went promptly to his room and started writing. After a few minutes I went to check on him. He was sitting on the floor writing with an agitated look on his face. I noticed that the verse he was writing was a lot longer than the Golden Rule. So I sat down beside him and asked, "Son, what verse are you writing?"

He snapped back, "The one you told me to write — Luke 15:21!"

Instead of writing the Golden Rule, he had written a verse from the parable of the Prodigal Son. It read: "Father, I have sinned against heaven and against you, I am no longer worthy to be called your son."

I couldn't help but laugh, put my arms around him and say, "Let's just forget the whole thing."

Now, we can apply the Golden Rule in one of three ways: a *give-and-take* style; a *pure-take style*; or a *pure-give* style.[15] Let me explain what I mean. The *give-and-take style* reflects a contract; that

is, we usually do no more or less for others than they do for us. We
love others when and because they love us. We fulfill the equity of
the relationship to the letter of the law. The *pure-take* style is one of
utter selfishness, narcissism and self-absorption. It says, Do to others so that they will do for you, or worse, Do to others before they do
to you. Only the *pure-give* style expresses covenant love.

Listen to Jesus' explanation of the *pure-give* kind of love:

*But I tell you who hear me: Love your enemies, do good to
those who hate you, bless those who curse you, pray for those
who mistreat you. If someone strikes you on the cheek, turn
to him the other also. If someone takes your cloak, do not
stop him from taking your tunic. Give to everyone who asks
you, and if anyone takes what belongs to you, do not demand
it back. Do to others as you would have them do to you. If you
love those who love you, what credit is that to you? Even
"sinners" love those who love them. And if you do good to
those who are good to you, what credit is that to you? Even
"sinners" do that. And if you lend to those from whom you
expect repayment, what credit is that to you? Even "sinners"
lend to "sinners," expecting to be repaid in full. But love your
enemies, do good to them, and lend to them without expecting to get anything back. Then your reward will be great, and
you will be sons of the Most High, because he is kind to the
ungrateful and wicked. Be merciful, just as your Father is
merciful. Do not judge, and you will not be judged. Do not
condemn, and you will not be condemned. Forgive, and you
will be forgiven. Give, and it will be given to you. A good
measure, pressed down, shaken together and running over,
will be poured into your lap. For with the measure you use it
will be measured to you.*[16]

Notice the paradoxical statements He makes: *love* your *enemies;*

do good to those who *hate* you; *bless* those who *curse* you; *pray* for those who *mistreat* you. Also note the statements which reflect an imbalance in a relationship:

If someone strikes your cheek, turn to him also the other.

If someone takes your cloak, do not stop him from taking your tunic.

If someone takes what belongs to you, do not demand it back.

Hey, that's not fair! we say. That may be true. But the fact of the matter is this, Jesus calls us to take the high road of covenant love — a love that does not reciprocate what others do to us but rather transcends what they may or may not do, even to the point that we overcome evil with good.

The demands may be great, but the return is out-of-this-world. Jesus promises, *"Give and it will be given to you."* He's not saying, "Give so that you will receive something in return." Such an admonition would be contractual. No, He means, "Give to give—without expectation or demand of something in return." Then He adds this incredible promise: *"It will be given to you. A good measure, pressed down, shaken together and running over will be poured into your lap."* The return will far outweigh the gift because we give purely for the sake of giving not receiving.

Now, I need to point out that sometimes such lavish giving is one-sided in a marriage. The wife gives but the husband doesn't, or vice versa. Selfless giving is not always rewarded by the recipient. The reward comes from God. He who sees what is done in secret will reward us openly.

This is not to suggest that a person is to remain in a marriage where there is negligence, abuse or cruelty. No person should submit himself or herself to abuse in any form. Such a notion is a distortion of unconditional love. I am talking about healthy marriages in which husbands and wives relate to each other without such notions of give-and-take, counting the cost or looking for the return. They give to each other because they love each other — plain and simple.

The concept of marriage as a covenant could be easily distorted to mean a passive, irresponsible relationship all in the name of unconditional love. Nothing could be further from the truth. Unconditional love does not act irresponsibly or take advantage of others. To the contrary—covenant love expresses itself in a solemn obligation to fulfill its vows and keeps its promises to the recipient of the covenant.

As Mother Theresa writes in *Garment of Love:*

Love has a hem to her garment
that reaches the very dust.
It sweeps the streets and lanes,
And because it can, it must.

WHEN WE FALL SHORT

All this talk about unconditional love sounds great, but what do we do when we break the covenant and don't keep our vows? To answer the question, we need to ask, How does God deal with us when we break our covenant with Him? When we sin, God doesn't terminate our relationship. Our unfaithfulness does not change His faithfulness. To the contrary, *"If we are faithless, He will remain faithful, for he cannot disown himself."*[17] This promise is one of the most profound statements in the entire Bible. Think of it—God is faithful to His covenant even when we are faithless!

When we break the covenant, God repairs the covenant and restores our relationship with Him. One Bible scholar points out that, "Man cannot annul the covenant if he breaks it...The majesty of divine love shows itself in this, that God alone has the power to dissolve the relationship, yet never makes use of it."[18]

What a beautiful thought—God has the power to dissolve the covenant but never makes use of that power. Why not? (Every one of us has given Him ample reason to do so.) Because He has insepara- bly bound Himself to us on oath in the covenant. As the Apostle Paul reminds us: *"I have become absolutely convinced that neither death nor life, neither messenger of Heaven nor monarch of earth, neither a power from on high nor a power from below, nor anything else in God's whole world has any power to separate us from the love of God in Christ Jesus our Lord!"*[19]

What do you think would happen to the divorce rate if husbands and wives loved each other like that? Instead of looking for justifi- able reasons for divorce, what if we overlooked each other's sins, forgave each other and never made use of our power to dissolve the covenant? Obviously, divorces would all but disappear. While a con- tract exists as a commercial or litigious binding of two parties, the covenant constitutes a relationship characterized by unconditional love which cannot be broken.

Everyone loves a love story. One of the most moving love stories in the Bible concerns an Old Testament prophet named Hosea and his wife, Gomer. Gomer left Hosea for a life of illicit affairs with other men. What was he to do? She stood to ruin his entire life and ministry. While logic said to divorce her and get a wife more suitable for the ministry, God told him to go find her and take her back.

As he searched the city, he finally located her at a slave auction. She had sold herself into slavery in order to financially survive. Jaded and used up in the market of "sex for sale," she was being auctioned off for only half the price of a common slave. No one even offered a bid for her. No one wanted her.

Suddenly, from the back of the crowd, she heard a familiar voice. "I'll take her," a man called out over the noisy crowd. She stood there stunned as he moved through the crowd toward her. She couldn't believe it. He refused to let her go even after all she'd done to hurt him. Can you picture them rushing into each other's arms? His love washed her clean and gave them a brand new life together.

Now for the punch line. God used their restored relationship to teach us about His love when we fail Him: *"I will heal their way-wardness and love them freely."*[20] The key words in God's promise are the words *heal* and *freely*. God's love given freely heals us of our sins, failures and shortcomings.

So it is with marriage. When a couple shares a covenant mar-riage they remain faithful in spite of failures, hurts and disappoint-ments. Such love overcomes all obstacles and opens the way for a joy too great for words in their lives.

Putting It Into Perspective

Let's summarize what we've learned about the covenant and how it transcends a contract.

CONTRACT	Versus	COVENANT
two-party agreement	versus	*one-party commitment*
conditional	versus	*unconditional love*
give-and-take	versus	*pure-give*
bargain	versus	*gift*
based on human effort	versus	*based on God's grace*
equality of resources	versus	*mutuality of resources*
love if / love because of	versus	*love in spite of*
expectations	versus	*sacrifice*
demands	versus	*freedom*
rights	versus	*self-surrender*
power struggles	versus	*mutual submission*

REFLECTIONS

Before reading any further, take a few minutes to reflect on your marriage. Are you operating on demands and expectations? Do you negotiate with each other to get what you want? Do you have a secret "wish list" of expectations which keeps you in a state of dissatisfaction with your partner?

Or, do you give yourselves freely to each other, no strings attached? When you experience disappointment or hurt, do you respond quickly with forgiveness or do you harbor resentment? Do you treat each other the way God treats you?

I admit that the covenant approach to marriage may sound too good to be true—maybe even beyond reach. It's certainly not the going trend of the day. But let me encourage you to rise above the spirit of the age that defines marriage as nothing more than a legal contract and take the high road of covenant living.

In the words of Robert Frost:

Two roads diverged in a wood, And I—
I took the one less traveled by,
And that has made all the difference.

CHAPTER THREE

WHO'S IN CHARGE?

THOMAS WHEELER, FORMER CEO OF THE MASSACHUSETTS MUTUAL Life Insurance Company, used to tell a charming story about himself. He and his wife were driving along an interstate when he noticed they were low on gas. Wheeler got off the highway at the next exit and soon found a run-down gas station with only one pump. He asked the attendant to fill the tank and check the oil, then went for a walk around the station to stretch his legs.

When he got back to the car he noticed his wife talking to the attendant like they were good friends. Their conversation ended as he paid the attendant. As they were getting in the car, he noticed the attendant wave to his wife and say, "It was great talking to you."

Driving out of the station Wheeler asked his wife if she knew the man. She admitted she did and went on to say that they had been high school sweethearts.

Feeling a bit jealous by this time Wheeler boasted, "You sure were lucky I came along." "If you had married him you'd be the wife of a gas station attendant instead of the wife of a chief executive officer."

"Sweetheart," she replied, "if I had married him, he'd be the chief executive officer and you'd be the gas station attendant."[1]

The important role women play in the home, the church and society at large has been downplayed long enough. Women want equal status with men and they deserve it. The Christian faith, above all religions, speaks for the equality of all people: *"There is neither Jew nor Greek, slave nor free, male nor female, for you are all one in Christ."*[2] Jesus did more to elevate the dignity of womanhood and to defend the rights of women than any person who has ever lived.

When Abraham Lincoln was seventeen years old, he sang a song at his sister's wedding that celebrated the glory of womanhood:

The woman was not taken
From Adam's feet we see;
So he must not abuse her
The meaning seems to be.
The woman was not taken
From Adam's head, we know;
To show she must not rule him —
'Tis evidently so.
The woman she was taken
From under Adam's arm;
So she must be protected
From injuries and harm.[3]

The power struggle between the sexes often takes place on the battlefield of marriage. One of the primary issues raised in defining Christian marriage centers around the concepts of authority and submission. These concepts are not only being explored and debated within the church but also within society at large involving several public policy debates, the most important being the Equal Rights Amendment.

The central issue at stake is authority: Who's in charge? "Should it rest with husband and father, as the orthodox and their culturally conservative allies prefer? Or should authority and responsibility be shared on egalitarian principles, as progressives and their liberal allies favor?"[4]

Within the Christian community there are those who strongly advocate the wife's submission to her husband in full recognition of his God-ordained role as the head of the household.[5] While the Bible clearly uses the language of submission, the implications of such submission in marriage require a more thorough examination than has been conducted to date. The problem we face is defining submission from a cultural rather than a biblical standpoint.

On the other hand, there are those who view submission as a call to partnership between a husband and his wife, characterized by mutual support, respect and cooperation as they manage the affairs of the home. Karl Barth points out that the tendency of men to dominate and the compliance of the woman are both wrong—they fall short of God's will. Healthy marriages are free from such power struggles. He goes on to describe marriage as a relationship involving a choice of love in which husbands and wives recognize, affirm and desire one another as partners for life.[6] The key word here is *partner.* Think about the implications of partnership. We'll come back to this idea in a minute.

So, what does the Bible really teach about God's order of authority in the home? To submit or not to submit—that is the question.

THE JESUS FACTOR

Although man exists as the head of the woman in God's creative order, his headship involves a submission to and a reflection of the headship of Jesus Christ. This means that husbands need to take their leadership cues from Jesus Himself. He showed us the way of true leadership in some very unique ways: by washing the feet of

His disciples, humbling Himself to the point of death and modeling a leadership style of servanthood.[7]

Jesus destroyed any notion that suggests a husband exercises full authority over his wife as the sole decision-maker in the marriage. He modeled the principle of shared authority by delegating His authority to His bride, the people of God and promising us a place of rulership on His eternal throne. While Jesus declared, *"All authority in heaven and on earth has been given to me,"* He also told His followers, *"I have given you authority."*[8] That's shared authority.

He also promises, *"To him who overcomes, I will give the right to sit with me on my throne just as I overcame and sat down with my Father on his throne."*[9] Since Jesus shares His authority with His bride, shouldn't husbands do the same with their wives? There's a big craze among Christian young people right now wearing some interesting wristbands and necklaces bearing the letters, "WWJD." It stands for, "What would Jesus do?" That's the real issue husbands must come to terms with — treating their wives with the same dignity and honor Jesus bestows on His bride, the church.

SUBMIT TO ONE ANOTHER

What's interesting is that the biblical teaching on submission involves both husbands and wives. The Apostle Paul writes, *"Submit to one another out of reverence for Christ."*[10] We've talked a long time in Christian circles about what it means for a wife to submit to her husband. It's time to raise another question: What does it mean for a husband to submit to his wife? That is, after all, exactly what Paul tells husbands to do.

The commandment for us to "submit to one another" marks the beginning of Paul's well-known passage on Christian marriage in Ephesians 5:21-33 and provides the backdrop for everything else he says about marriage and family living. Only after he calls us to mutual submission does he go on to say, *"Wives, submit to your husbands."*

Now let me share something with you that I find extremely interesting about this passage, as I think you will. The verb *submit* does not appear in the actual verse in many of the ancient manuscripts. So the statement actually reads, *"Wives, to your husbands."* Why would the word *submit* be left out of the sentence? Because the statement derives the verb from the preceding verse which, of course, calls for mutual submission. This means that submitting to one another forms the heart and soul of a healthy marriage and a happy family. Anything less is a relationship characterized by endless power struggles as one party tries to dominate and control the other.

Let's take a closer look at the meaning of submission. The word *submit* occurs 23 times in Paul's letters and means to submit to another person because of their inherent qualities or because of the position they hold.[11] He goes on to tell us that the reason a wife submits to her husband is *"out of reverence for Christ."* Which means, that a wife's submission to her husband is not forced or coerced but rather voluntary. Or, to use Paul's words, *"as to the Lord."* She honors God as she fulfills her vows of love to her husband.

As opposed to being a harsh, overbearing command, *"Wives, submit,"* it is a beautiful metaphor of the most sublime imagery comparing Christian marriage to the relationship of Christ and His church. The Bible also says that wives are also called to love their husbands and to respect them.[12] I point this out because I have actually heard it said that nowhere in the New Testament are wives told to love their husbands, only to submit to them. This simply isn't the case. Besides, what would submission be worth if not accompanied by love?

There are two kinds of submission. First, there is submission which is forced, coerced and manipulated. Such submission is completely unChristian. Then there is submission based on love. This is why Paul goes on to say that a wife desires to submit to her husband because he loves her *"as Christ loved the church and gave himself up for her."* Without such love there can be no real submission in marriage.

So, let's deal with the real question at hand: How can a husband submit to his wife? Simply by loving her as Christ loves the church. The Apostle Peter puts it this way: *"Husbands be considerate of your wives and treat them with respect as the weaker partner and as heirs with you of the gracious gift of life."*[13] He uses the words *partner* and *heirs* intentionally; they're covenant words. As opposed to being a hierarchy of authoritarian roles, Christian marriage exists as a partnership of shared responsibilities and privileges under the kingly rule of Jesus Christ.

As far back as the fourth century A.D. the church struggled to sort out the meaning of marriage as a partnership. Ambrose, bishop of Milan wrote: "A woman must respect her husband, not be a slave to him; she consents to be ruled, not to be forced. The one whom a yoke would fit is not for the yoke of marriage. As to man, he should guide his wife like a pilot, honor her as a partner in life, share with her as a co-heir of grace."[14]

Mutual submission creates an atmosphere of peace, humility and servanthood at home. John Chrysostom, presbyter at Antioch in the late fourth century and later bishop of Constantinople, describes this partnership:

For there is nothing which so welds our life together as the love of man and wife. For this many will lay aside even their arms, for this they will give up life itself, and Paul would never without reason and without an object have spent so much pains on this subject, as when he says here, "Wives, be in subjection to your own husbands, as to the Lord." And why so? Because when they are in harmony, the children are well brought up, and the domestics are in good order, and neighbors, and friends, and relatives enjoy the fragrance. But if it be otherwise, all is turned upside down, and thrown into confusion.[15]

While their roles may differ, a husband and wife live together as covenant partners who stand on equal ground. (Only when you see your partner as God's gift to you can you fully accept and respect him or her and discover the joy of mutual submission.)

SPIRITUAL LEADERSHIP

We need to turn our attention to the issue of spiritual leadership in marriage. I'm sure you've probably heard somewhere along the line that the husband is suppose to be the spiritual leader of the home. The Bible certainly underscores this vital role for husbands. Homes today are in desperate need of men who will take their place as spiritual leaders. Men who will build an altar and worship God like Abraham. Men who will intercede for their children like Job. Men who can honestly say with Joshua of old, *"As for me and my house we will serve the Lord."*

As both a husband and a father I honestly seek to fulfill my role of spiritual leadership in our home by serving my wife and children. But, am I the only spiritual leader in our home? Isn't my wife also, by virtue of her relationship to God, a spiritual leader in partnership with me? Sure she is. Let me share with you one of the most profound truths found in the entire Bible—that all believers are priests before God. The Bible says, *"you are a royal priesthood...a people belonging to God,"* and that Christ *"has made us to be a kingdom and priests to serve his God and Father."*[16] Did you know that you are a priest before God? Well, you are.

We call this the priesthood of all believers. Now, what happens to the idea that the husband/ father is the sole priest of his home when we compare it with the priesthood of all believers? To put it frankly, it comes unraveled. Since a wife is also a priest before God we cannot speak of husbands as "the priest" of the home. The spiritual priesthood of the home resides with both the husband and his wife.

Now follow me closely. I am not saying that the husband is not a priest in his home—he is. I am only underscoring the fact that he is not the *only* priest in the home—his wife also serves as a priest. This priesthood clearly defines marriage as a partnership in which they share the spiritual leadership of their home together.

Let's talk more about what it means to be a priest. In the Bible we see the Old Testament priests fulfilling a two-fold ministry. First, they minister to God in worship and in intercessory prayer for others. Second, they minister to people's needs and teach the word of God. The Latin word for priest, *pontifex,* means "a bridge-builder." That's what a priest does; he builds bridges to God for others to cross. That is what Jesus did for us when He died on the cross for our sins and rose on the third day. He built a bridge of love by which we can be reconciled to God.

So, you can see that any husband who boldly asserts his authority to his wife by announcing, "I'm the head of the home and you need to submit to my decision" is on a collision course with disaster. He's much better off to say to his wife, "We are covenant partners together. Let's pray about the situation we're facing and trust God to speak to us." Men need to be humble enough to receive the counsel of their wives with as much enthusiasm as they want their wives to show when they share their views with them.

Let's re-cap what we've learned about spiritual leadership at home. First, every believer is a priest before God. This means that leadership is shared by a husband and wife as equal partners in the covenant. Second, while the husband certainly fulfills a God-appointed role as a spiritual leader, he is not the sole source of that leadership. His wife shares that leadership with him. The truly wise husband will recognize her spiritual leadership in the home and elevate her to a place of equal partnership.

THE SERVANT STYLE

Submitting to one another also means to serve one another in love. All this talk about who's in charge needs to be replaced with the language of love. True love serves. Jesus taught that in the kingdom of God authority means service; it doesn't mean control, power or position. Interestingly enough, His own disciples struggled with this issue. On one occasion, Jesus seized the opportunity to drive home the point that spiritual authority serves others.

> *Then James and John, the sons of Zebedee, came to him. "Teacher," they said, "we want you to do for us whatever we ask." "What do you want me to do for you?" he asked. They replied, "Let one of us sit at your right and the other at your left in your glory." When the ten heard about this, they became indignant with James and John. Jesus called them together and said, "You know that those who are regarded as rulers of the Gentiles lord it over them, and their high officials exercise authority. Not so with you. Instead, whoever wants to become great among your must be your servant, and whoever wants to be first must be slave of all. For even the Son of Man did not come to be served, but to give his life as a ransom for many."*[17]

Disturbing, isn't it? James and John were so bent on political power that they actually had the audacity to ask Jesus for the two top positions in His kingdom. What were they really asking for?

Didn't they want to rule over the other disciples? That's exactly what they wanted. You can understand why the rest of the disciples were furious with them.

So, to clear up the matter, Jesus defined authority in one profound statement: *"Whoever wants to become great among you must be your servant, and whoever wants to be first must be slave of all."* In the kingdom of God, authority means servanthood—plain and simple. When the Bible teaches that a husband has been given authority by God in the home, it means that God has appointed him to serve his wife and children just as Jesus serves the church—service measured by a cross.

As you can see, there is a world of difference between human authority and spiritual authority. The former stands upright in pride, while the latter bows down in humility.

Servanthood brings a spiritual dimension to love. Without spiritual love we seek to absorb others into our own personality and to dominate them. Such human love forces another, consciously or unconsciously, into one's sphere of influence and power. Spiritual love, however, refrains from controlling, manipulating or using others, and in turn allows them to be free. True love releases others to become what God wants them to be.

Perhaps this poem entitled, *Letting Go,* says it best:

To let go doesn't mean to stop caring,
*   it means I can't do it for someone else.*
To let go is not to cut myself off,
*   it's the realization that I can't control another.*
To let go is not to enable,
*   but to allow learning from natural consequences.*
To let go is to admit powerlessness,
*   which means the outcome is not in my hands.*

To let go is not to try to change or blame another,
    I can only change myself.
To let go is not to care for,
    but to care about.
To let go is not to fix,
    but to be supportive.
To let go is not to judge,
    but to allow another to be a human being.
To let go is not to be in the middle arranging all the outcomes,
    but to allow others to effect their own outcomes,
To let go is not to be protective;
    it is to permit another to face reality.
To let go is not to deny,
    but to accept.
To let go is not to nag, scold, or argue,
    but to search out my own shortcomings and to correct them.
To let go is not to adjust everything to my desires,
    but to take each day as it comes.
To let go is not to criticize and regulate anyone,
    but to try to become what dream I can be.
To let go is not to regret the past,
    but to grow and live for the future.
To let go is to fear less and love more!

Author Unknown

LIVING ON THE EDGE

Covenant love not only involves mutual submission and partnership, it even goes to the extreme of sacrificing the self for the good of another. The Hebrew verb, *karat,* meaning "to cut or to divide," stresses the sacrificial custom connected with the ancient rite of covenant-making. There can be no covenant without sacrifice. Covenant love is love on a cross. Now you can see what this command-ment really means: *"Husbands love your wives as Christ loved the church and gave himself up for her."*[18]

Love means self-sacrifice. So, while we're often preoccupied with what's going on with our partner and what we wish they would change, the greater issue we face is, What are you going to do with yourself?

The Greek philosophers said, "Know yourself."

Shakespeare said, "Be true to yourself."

The Eastern mystic says, "Transcend yourself."

The humanist says, "Actualize yourself."

The hedonist says, "Enjoy yourself."

The materialist says, "Fulfill yourself."

The motivational psychologist says, "Assert yourself."

The evolutionist says, "Create yourself."

Then Jesus walks by and says, *"Deny yourself..."* Now, don't get me wrong, the self is important. We all need a sense of self-esteem and a healthy self-image in order to live balanced lives. But to place the self at the center of one's life around which the whole world is expected to revolve results in pure selfishness. And that's the pri-mary problem couples are facing today — selfishness. Tragically, some people focus more on fulfilling the self than they do serving others.

As Peter Yarrow points out: "In the 1940's and 1950's we had the all-encompassing *Life* magazine. Then we cropped our vision down to *People* in the 70's. Things tightened up even more with *Us.* Next came *Self.* Somewhere there's got to be a magazine just for you: *Fred Morgenstein Monthly."*

Self-centeredness is public enemy number-one to married couples. Our psychiatrists tell us that narcissism is the leading personality disorder of our times. Narcissism derives its name from the Greek mythological character Narcissus, the son of Cephalus, the river god. He became obsessed with his own reflection in a pool of water. There he would sit for hours staring at his reflection. His self-obsession was so great that he rejected the love of the nymph Echo as well as the companionship of his friends. One day he leaned over to kiss his reflection and drowned in the pool.

The narcissist is a person who cares deeply about what others think; is on a quest to discover himself; needs constant affirmation and attention without which he becomes depressed or even paranoid; is overly dependent on others; is desperately insecure in himself or herself; is overly concerned with his or her public image which is projected as one of self-confidence while inwardly they feel inadequate; is obsessed with what this person meant by what he said or what this event means to them; is constantly searching for more— more personal meaning, more out of relationships, more out of life; lives for the moment with little or no concern for the historical past and no real plan for the future; and always asks, What am I getting out of it? Psychologists tell us that the narcissistic culture characteristic of America today focuses more on therapy than religion and on personal well-being than salvation.[19]

The answer to narcissism is the call of Jesus to deny yourself. Only then can you discover and develop your best self. Its a paradox that works!

We die to live.

We surrender to win.

We lose to find.

We serve to reign.

We give to receive.

So, permit me to ask you: Is there anything in your life that you need to deny so that your marriage can really blossom? What about unhealthy communication styles that block intimacy? Attitudes, values, beliefs or behaviors that are eroding your relationship? If so, surrender them to God in prayer. And then begin to make the changes you need to make so your marriage can flourish.

The art of sacrificial giving is the essence of mature love. Several years ago some friends of mine sold every material possession they owned to raise enough money to go the Philippines as missionaries. During their first year of ministry they rediscovered what it means to deny the self for the sake of others. They sent me the following Filipino parable entitled, *The Broken Bamboo* that shows us the way out of ourselves:

Once upon a time, in the heart of Mindanao lay a beautiful garden. The loveliest and most beloved of the plants in the garden was a gracious and noble bamboo. Stately in beauty, he danced to the delight of his master.

One day the Master visited the garden and looked upon the beloved bamboo with eyes of expectation. The bamboo in turn bowed his head in loving adoration. "Bamboo, bamboo, I need you. I would use you for something." The bamboo flung his head to the sky in delight. The day had come for which he had been made, the day for which he had been growing, the day of his destiny. "Master, I am ready. Use me as you wish."

"Bamboo, I will take and cut you down." A trembling of great horror shook the bamboo. "Cut me down? But you have made me the most beautiful in the garden! Oh, no, not that. Use me for your joy, O Master, but please don't cut me down." "My dear bamboo, if I cannot cut you down, I cannot use you," said the Master. The wind held its breath. The garden grew still. The bamboo bent his head and whispered, "Use me, but if you need to cut me down, do as you will and cut."

"Bamboo, my dear bamboo, I could cut your leaves and branches, too," said the Master again. "Master, Master, spare

me. Cut me down and lay my beauty in the dust...but should you take from me my leaves and branches?" "Bamboo, if I cannot cut them away I cannot use you." The sun hid his face. A listening butterfly glided fearfully away. The bamboo shivered in terrible expectancy, whispering low. "Master, cut right away." And the Master cut the branches away.

"Bamboo, bamboo, I would yet split you in half and cut your heart, for if I cannot do so, I cannot use you." Then the bamboo bowed to the ground. "Master, Master, then cut and split me in half." And the Master proceeded to cut the bamboo and split him in half. The Master carried the bamboo across the barren field. He arrived near the brook and started fixing it to the waterfall. Then, putting one end of the broken bamboo in the spring and the other end into the water channel in his field, the Master lay the bamboo down gently. The bubbling spring waters sang welcome! And the clear sparkling waters raced joyously down the channel of the bamboo's broken body into the waiting fields. Then, the Master planted some rice. And he waited. Then the field grew fertile and the rice started to grow.

On that day a deep joy touched the soul of the bamboo. Once he was so glorious in his beauty. Now he was even more glorious in his brokenness and humility. For in his beauty, he had life abundant, but in his brokenness, he became the channel of abundant life for his Master's field.

PARTNERS FOR LIFE

From the beginning of time God intended for a husband and his wife to live together as covenant partners for life — a partnership characterized by mutual love, respect and honor. That's what the biblical phrase, "they will become one flesh," really means. Herein lies the answer to the power struggle seen in so many marriages today.

The question is, Are you truly partners in your...

Decisions?

Authority?

Leadership?

Are you letting go of the control of each other's...

Personalities?

Development?

Goals and ambitions?

Are you denying your...

Unrealistic expectations?

Overbearing demands?

Selfish ambitions?

God's answer to the power struggle is a simple command of love: *"Submit to one another out of reverence for Christ."*

CHAPTER FOUR

CARING ENOUGH TO COMMUNICATE

L ET'S BE HONEST ABOUT IT: A MARRIAGE IS ONLY AS GOOD AS THE quality of communication between a husband and his wife. Sometimes a couple in crisis will remark, "The problem with our marriage is we just don't communicate!" The truth is, however, we cannot *not* communicate. We either communicate effectively or ineffectively, but we do communicate.

It's like the story about a lady who went to a judge to get a divorce. The judge asked her, "On what grounds do you want this divorce?"

She responded, "I have two acres of land—pick one."

The judge then inquired, "Lady, do you have a grudge?"

She replied, "No, we park in the front yard."

The judge, trying desperately to communicate with her, said, "Lady, does your husband beat you up?"

She said, "No, I always get up first."

Exasperated, the judge said, "Why do you want this divorce?"

The lady responded, "Because we just can't communicate!"

What is communication? Communication is a dynamic process

of interaction between two or more people involving talking, listening and understanding. Or, more simply put, it is conversation with a purpose.

TAMING THE TONGUE

Washington Irvine was right when he said, "The tongue is the only tool that grows sharper with constant use." With our tongues we can either bless or curse, heal or wound, build-up or tear down. Because of his words, Mark Anthony was called the silver-tongued orator of Rome. Because of his words, Abraham Lincoln was called the great emancipator. Because of his words, Winston Churchill was called the statesman of the century. Because of his words, Martin Luther King was called the voice of equality. Because of his words, Billy Graham is regarded as the greatest evangelist of the twentieth century. Because of her words, Mother Theresa was known as the defender of the weak.

Words are powerful. The Bible underscores the power of our words:[1]

"Reckless words pierce like a sword, but the tongue of the wise brings healing."

"A gentle answer turns away wrath, but a harsh word stirs up anger."

"The power of life and death is in the tongue."

"He who guards his mouth and his tongue keeps himself from calamity."

"Be quick to listen, slow to speak and slow to become angry."

Here's my favorite: *"Do not let any unwholesome talk come out of your mouths, but only what is helpful for building others up according to their needs, that it may benefit those who listen."*[2] What a challenge for any relationship, especially marriage.

It is estimated that we engage in about 30 conversations per day and that the average person spends one-fifth of his or her lifetime talking, which equals out to about 13 years. (Some people are trying to get it all in at one time!) Every year we speak enough words to write 132 books each containing 400 pages!

James Dobson humorously points out that men and women differ on the amount of words they use every day. While the average man speaks about 25,000 words a day, the average woman speaks about 50,000 words. The problem occurs when a husband gets home in the evening he has already used up 24,999 words and grunts his way through the evening. But she's got another 25,000 words to go!

While words are certainly powerful, the non-verbal side of communication is equally powerful — and complex! First, there is *the actual message versus the implied meaning*. You could say to your partner, "I love you." But how you say it is as important, if not more important. You can say, "I love you," with a note of sincerity and gentleness, or you could say, "I love you," with a non-chalant or coy attitude. So when we communicate, there are the actual words spoken and the underlying message.

There is also a mixture of the *verbal message versus the non-verbal message*. Body language, eye contact, tone of voice and facial expressions all play a vital part in the process of communication.

THREE LEVELS OF COMMUNICATION

When couples complain about poor communication what they typically mean is that their communication lacks depth, emotional openness and intimacy. The goal of marriage is to learn to communicate at this deeper, emotional level. All communication takes place on one of three levels.

Surface-level communication. We exchange clichés or talk about events or other people but don't reveal anything about ourselves in the dialogue. We make no emotional investment. Complete strangers can even communicate on a surface level. Two people pass on the street. One says to the other, "How are you doing today?" The other responds, "Fine." They have exchanged colloquialisms but aren't any closer to each other for having met.

Situation-level communication. This level is a bit more involved than the first. Instead of simply exchanging clichés we talk about personal issues that are important to us such as making family decisions, managing finances or raising the kids. Many couples never move beyond this stage. While it is certainly important that couples talk openly about the situations they face, they still have not revealed themselves to each other at this level.

Self-disclosure level communication. The deepest and most meaningful form of communication is what we call "gut-level" communication which means sharing on an emotional level. Self-disclosure means you make yourself fully known to another person. It requires the willingness to be emotionally vulnerable as we make ourselves completely transparent, honest and open. Couples achieve true intimacy when they open up to each other and share the way they feel. No masks or facades. No hiding from each other. Honesty is the key. An emotional investment takes place in the process. Intimacy is more than sexual love, it is the emotional sharing of ourselves together in a relationship of trust and unconditional love. I recall hearing Naomi Judd speaking at the memorial service for Tammy Wynette define intimacy as, "into me you see." That's about the best definition I've heard to date on this thing called intimacy — into me you see.

Sounds great, but how is it done? First, *identify your feelings.* You can't share your feelings unless you've identified those feelings. Often we are out of touch with our feelings. We bury our feelings, deny them or mask them in an effort to avoid becoming exposed emotionally. Sometimes we are uncomfortable sharing our feelings.

We prefer to talk about what we think. It's less risky than sharing how we feel. So we say such things as, "I feel confused." Notice how the words feel and confused are connected. Confusion, however, is a mental state not an emotional state. But, again, we are more comfortable saying what we think than what we feel. Work on identifying your feelings. Make a list of feeling words like anger, hurt, fear, joy, disappointment, and so forth so that you can become comfortable explaining how you feel.

Next, *report your feelings.* When you've clearly identified your feelings you're ready to share them with your partner. And make sure you use these "feeling words." Also, remember to choose the right timing, the right setting and the right manner before you get into a heavy conversation, especially, if you're angry or hurt. Failure to do so often results in serious conflicts and misunderstanding.

When you share how you feel remember to *own your feelings.* Don't blame your partner for the way you feel. Take responsibility for your feelings. The most potentially dangerous word we use in conversations is the word *you.* Immediately the listener gets defensive. So begin with the words "I feel" instead of, "You make me feel." When you say, "I feel," you demonstrate ownership of your emotions and it takes the heat off your partner. He or she then knows you're not blaming them for the way you feel. Also, try to avoid such phrases as "you *always*..." or "you *never*..." when confronting your partner. Such negative generalizations result in conflict or hurt feelings and keep you from dealing with the real issues you need to talk about.

Finally, *resolve your feelings.* When you follow this simple path of identifying feelings, owning feelings and then openly sharing feelings you are able to resolve any conflicts you may have had. Your marriage will grow to a new level of understanding and openness.

GAMES PEOPLE PLAY

There are also some serious barriers to healthy communication we need to expose. We could call these barriers "games people play" which are nothing short of the way we try to control others and to exercise power. Whether we like it or not all relationships, especially marriage, deal with issues of control. We vie for power and try to get our way; we often hide our true feelings and shut out the people we love so they won't get too close. The list of games are endless but here are some we need to look out for:

Explosion. The explosive personality likes to control others by yelling, slamming doors and a variety of behaviors by which they show their hostility. They can easily fly off the handle, have rage reactions or throw temper tantrums to get everybody in the house to take notice and to conform to their wishes. And don't bother confronting them about their behavior — they'll only become more defensive and demonstrative. The goals of the game include keeping people from getting too close or winning by intimidation. The bad news is it works. Everyone in the house ends up walking on egg shells out of fear and giving into their demands just to try to keep the peace. That is, until someone takes all he or she can and decides they won't take it anymore and leaves. Obviously, such immature behavior prohibits any chance for open communication in any marriage or family. Most people would rather keep their thoughts to themselves and hide their feelings than face such intimidating outbursts of rage.

Silence. This is the same game as the explosion game except that the anger is masked instead of being openly expressed. You never know where you stand with the person who gives you the silent treatment. They freeze you out. We call it passive-aggressive behavior. While you know he or she is angry, they don't express their anger openly. Instead, they ignore you, or gossip about you behind your back or lie to you. Again, the goal is power and control in the relationship. If you ask them, "What's wrong?" They feel very justified in saying, "Nothing." And usually with a coy tone of voice all the while letting you know by their non-verbal expressions that there is something seriously wrong. But they keep you guessing. This behavior is just as destructive in a marriage as explosive behaviors.

Criticism. While there is surely a place in marriage for correction, constant criticism of one's partner comes off as intimidation and domination. "I wish you would wear your hair differently." Or, "I wish you would dress like Susan at the office." Or, "take the leadership of our home like Bill does with his family." On and on the litany of unfair comparisons and criticisms goes. Sadly, we often seek to elevate ourselves by putting someone else down. I once read that the only deserved criticism is a better deed. We would all be better off if that was the only kind of criticism we gave. Criticism comes from several sources. Sometimes we criticize others innocently in an effort to help them make improvements we think they need to make. Criticism can just be an act of meanness and cruelty. Criticism can also be an expression of discontentment and unhappiness in marriage. Whatever the source, realize the incredibly destructive power of criticism and commit yourself to being an encourager rather than a critic.

Endless chatter. Healthy relationships are characterized by a balance between talking and listening. Constant talking by one person keeps the other from sharing what they think and how they feel. It's like the story I heard about a farmer who died. The preacher who was to conduct the funeral was somewhat unfamiliar with the family. So, before the service, he visited the farm to learn about the farmer who died. He asked the farmer's son, "Did your father have any last words before he died?" "Oh, no sir," the boy replied. "Mama was with him right up till the end."

When Barbie and I first got married, someone showed us a silly game to play to make sure everyone gets a chance to speak. It's called the spoon game. Here's how you play it: Take a simple spoon. The person who is holding the spoon gets to speak and only that person. The other person has to listen attentively without saying a word. When the first person gets finished they have to surrender the spoon and reverse roles. Believe me its an excellent exercise in helping break such habits as failing to listen attentively, interrupting others when they speak and talking too much.

Let me share this short course in communication with you before we go on to discuss how to develop good listening skills.

1. The 6 most important words: *I admit I made a mistake*.
2. The 5 most important words: *You did a good job*.
3. The 4 most important words: *What is your opinion?*
4. The 3 most important words: *If you please*
5. The 2 most important words: *Thank you*
6. The most important word: *We*
7. The least important word: *I*

Listen Up!

Listening is one of the most important skills for success in any relationship, especially marriage. Peter Drucker, the father of American management, claims that 60 percent of all management problems are a result of ineffective communications.

Listening is hard work. It requires giving someone your undivided attention, focusing on what is being said both verbally and non-verbally, shutting out distractions and trying to see the issue from the other person's perspective without getting defensive or preparing a rebuttal. Remember to always face the person who is talking to you, maintain eye-contact and tune in to what is being said. Active listening is one of the most important ways that we show love and respect to others. "Rapt and exclusive attention," says Robert

Fisher, "is one of the greatest gifts we can give another individual. It is the highest form of compliment."[3]

What does it really mean to listen to someone?

L stands for love; I care about you and your concerns.

I stands for integrity; I am safe to talk to; I am trustworthy.

S stands for stay on track; receive and accept the message as it is sent.

T stands for tune in; active listening; body language reflects a listening posture.

E stands for emotion; I listen for what you feel not simply what you say.

N stands for non-judgmental love; I value what you say; avoid defensiveness, generalizations and judgmentalism; and don't respond by saying, "You shouldn't feel that way."

It pays to listen. James Lynch in, *The Language of the Heart,* conducted research on the dynamics of communication from a physiological standpoint. He observed several important principles. First, when we talk, our blood-pressure and heart-rate rises rapidly. This is even true for deaf-mute persons when they sign. For people who are hypertensive the rise is much greater than for normal people — often rising to the level of a danger zone. Hypertensive people often fail to listen; are on guard and defensive; talk intensely; talk over others; as a result their pressure stays up. He also found that listening lowers blood pressure. Undefensive listening in hypertensive people significantly lowers their pressure.[4]

When listening, remember to hear the person out before jumping to conclusions. We have a tendency to interrupt or make rash responses. We need to be patient, to think with our brains not our tongues and to weigh carefully what is being said. As the proverb goes, *"He who answers before listening, that is his folly and shame."*[5]

Not only is the content of what is being said important, so is the context. Ask, is your husband or wife tired, moody, angry or frustrated? Are they simply under too much stress at work? Everybody has a bad day every now and then and sometimes say things we don't mean. At those times, the best thing we can do as good listeners is simply allow our partner to vent their feelings, within proper limits, and to lovingly respond, "I understand how you feel."

DECODING THE MESSAGE

Sorting through the maze of emotions, body language, tone of voice, hidden agendas and the games we play can be overwhelming. I think you'll enjoy the following guide to help you decode what men and women really mean when they say certain things.[6]

When She Says...	She really means
We need...	I want...
Do what you want.	You'll pay for this later.
Sure...go ahead.	I don't want you to do that.
The kitchen is so inconvenient.	I want a new home.
The trash is full.	Take it out now!
Nothing is wrong.	Everything is wrong.
I don't want to talk about it.	Go away. I'm still building up steam.
Am I fat?	Tell me I'm beautiful.
You have to learn to communicate.	Just agree with me.
Are you listening?	Too late. You're dead.

When he says....	He really means...
Boy, am I hungry!	Make me something to eat and serve me on the couch.
It's too expensive.	You could get a neat computer for that!
It's a beautiful day.	It's too hot to do yard work.
I have a surprise.	I bought something stupid.
Why don't you get a job?	You bought something really stupid.
You can't mow the lawn when the grass is wet.	There's a game on the TV.

Advice for husbands. Most men would benefit greatly from increasing their listening skills. We have a tendency to want to hurry our wives up when they're telling us something. "Hurry up, honey," we say, "spare me the details and get to the bottom line." Women tend to like to talk about details which men think are unimportant. Husbands need to learn to take time and listen to details. Not because the details are important but because *she's* important! Remember, listening is love. We listen to the people we care about.

It's like the wife who came in the house one day and said to her husband, "Sweetheart, the car won't start."

He asked, "What's wrong with it?"

She said, "There's water in the carburetor."

He exclaimed, "Water in the carburetor? That's impossible! Besides you don't even know what a carburetor is. Where's the car?"

She said, "It's in the swimming pool!"

The biggest mistake husbands make is thinking that their wives want their expert opinion on everything. As humbling as it may be, that's usually the farthest thing from the truth. All they want is for them to listen. When a man's wife sits him down and says, "I have something I want to share with you," she's not asking him to fix the problem. Now I know that this will come as a shock to many men. But it's the truth. She only wants him to give her his undivided attention and listen. Why? Because listening shows that you care.

This point was driven home to me during a marriage seminar that Barbie and I conducted some time ago. We gave the couples a communication exercise. Each person was asked to write down what he or she needed from their partner to improve their communication. Even though we were leading the seminar we completed the exercises along with the group. I have to admit that I was a little bit shocked by what Barbie said she needed from me: (1) to listen more, (2) to avoid the know-it-all attitude (that's advice giving), and (3) to give her more encouragement. I got the point — she was asking for me to listen and understand her, not to fix every problem.

Not only does a wife need her husband to listen empathically, she also needs to feel free to share her opinions and viewpoints. The truly wise husband knows that the key to his wife's heart is making her feel like she's the most important person in the world to him. That's when intimate communication begins to take place.

Advice for wives. Men usually want to get right to the bottom line and then make a quick decision. So when they listen they are usually thinking about what they can do to fix the problem. It is important for women to know that men find joy in providing for their wives and in solving problems for them. Some will criticize such actions as male chauvinism — demeaning a woman's ability to solve the problem herself. Personally, I think that the efforts of husbands to help out is motivated by love. So wives need to indulge their husbands at times by allowing them to offer advice or solve the problem. It's a way men show love.

On a more humorous note, women need to bear in mind that men suffer from short attention spans when it comes to listening to endless details — unless they're watching Monday Night Football for three hours. All kidding aside, it would be helpful if men and women could meet half-way on this point. Men need to learn to listen more to details without trying to get to the bottom line. And women would do well to work on giving the *Reader's Digest* condensed version when talking to their husbands.

Wives also need to remember that men like to talk about details when it comes to something that is important to them. The difference is that men tend to share detailed information much like a news reporter — brief, utilitarian and to the point. When a wife listens to her husband he feels significant. While women report a high need for security in marriage, men need to feel significant, held in high esteem by their wives.

A couple were attending a party chatting with friends when the subject of marriage counseling came up. "Oh, we'll never need that. Bob and I have a great relationship," the wife explained. "He was a communications major in college and I majored in theater arts. He communicates real well and I act like I'm listening."

Becky Freeman gives some insightful advice for wives: "Men don't stop talking because they aren't 'talkers' by nature. They stop talking because we stop listening. They stop talking because their attempts at conversation are met with our criticism. We tease them about their subject choice or judge them or interrupt them with our views."[7]

Listening is an art we all need to master. The following listening ladder is helpful:

L — Look at the person
A — Ask questions
D — Don't interrupt
D — Don't change the subject
E — Empathize
R — Respond verbally and non-verbally

COMPLETING THE COMMUNICATION LOOP

Communication is only complete when we understand each other. The ultimate goal of talking and listening is to understand and to be understood. "When someone deeply listens to you," writes poet John Fox, "it is like holding out a dented cup you've had since childhood and watching it fill up with cold, fresh water. When it balances on top of the brim, you are understood. When it overflows and touches your skin, you are loved."[8]

FIGHTING FAIR

Whether we like it or not, conflict is an inevitable part of any relationship. Convictions clash. Disagreements occur. Tempers flare. Feelings get hurt. We say things we wish we had never said. We blow situations out of proportion. We jump to conclusions. It's all part of being married. Healthy communication doesn't require the absence of conflict but rather the ability to resolve it productively so that we end up better not bitter.

Consider a simple object lesson from physics. Take your hands and move them close together. What do you feel? Warmth, right? Now, rub your hands back and forth together. The warmth intensifies because you generate friction. So, when any two objects move against each other, friction is created which, in turn, generates heat.

The same is true of people. When any two people, with their unique personalities, likes and dislikes, come together, they generate friction, both positively and negatively. Granted, some people generate more friction than others, but all couples experience friction at some level. Positively, we generate love and passion and intimacy. Negatively, we disagree, argue and compete. The only way to avoid friction is to stay away from each other. But, if we do, we are left with detached marriages that lack intimacy and openness. The price of closeness is the willingness to run the risk of getting hurt — of experiencing occasional friction and conflict in marriage. The same closeness that brings you joy will also produce conflict. You can't have one without the other. Unfortunately, some couples settle for a surface relationship in an effort to avoid conflict at all costs. The problem is, when you avoid conflict, you might also avoid closeness.

Let's take a closer look at the ups and downs of conflict in marriage. Conflict isn't necessarily bad in a relationship. To be sure, constant conflict is a sign that something is seriously wrong in a marriage. But occasional run-ins, in a civilized manner I might add, can afford couples the opportunity to work through important issues that might lie buried beneath the surface and grow closer as a result. So, when conflict arises, stop and ask, "What can we learn from this experience to make our relationship better?" The goal of conflict is to use it as an opportunity for productive growth in your marriage.

The question comes, Why do couples fight? Couples experience conflict for three primary reasons. First, we attack each other by generalizations, confrontations and criticism. Second, we misunderstand something that is said or done by our partner. Third, unfinished business from the past, such as repressed resentments or unsettled issues, builds up with increased intensity until we finally blow.

The crucial issue is, How can we resolve conflict when it arises? Let me give some down-to-earth suggestions:

1. *Learn your dance.* What I mean by the term dance is the predictable pattern of conflict. One person usually does or says something which invariably leads the other one to respond a certain way. They exchange verbal blows until the situation escalates to the point of an emotional outburst or withdrawal from each other. It doesn't take long until couples can sense an argument coming. They go through the same basic steps every time they argue. Their dance is predictable. So, the first step in changing the pattern is to recognize the dance and the particular role each one plays in the process.

2. *Alter your typical response.* Now that you can know what causes your conflicts, it's time to select a new routine. That simply means to stop responding in the same old, predictable way that you have done in the past. The first time you do it will throw your partner for a loop. He or she won't have the foggiest notion of what to do next. Your new response will force him or her to reevaluate their own responses and make new choices. You can derail many potential conflicts before they even get started by changing your old responses for newer, more productive ones.

3. *Turn the other cheek.* You don't have to lash out or strike back at every criticism, hurtful actions or insensitive words by your partner. Overlook their mistakes. Hopefully, they will realize they've

said the wrong thing or responded incorrectly and apologize as a result of you keeping your peace. Remember the proverb, *"A soft answer turns away wrath, but a harsh word stirs up anger."* The words of Jesus are invaluable on this point: *"Turn the other cheek."* Remember, love covers a multitude of sins.

4. ***Be specific, not vague, when making requests.*** Conflict often occurs because we are vague when making a request. We expect our partner to be a mind-reader and automatically know what we want or need. When they don't deliver, we get our feelings hurt. So, when you make a request, be specific. Instead of saying, "Why don't you ever spend time with me?" Say, "I would like to spend more time with you on the weekends." This is especially important for wives when making requests of their husbands. Men are often clueless when a wife makes a request like, "Show me more often that you love me." That doesn't register with him. She's better off saying something like, "Take me out to dinner, a movie and bring me a dozen roses this Friday evening." Now he knows what she means. Remember, be specific not vague.

5. ***Be positive, not negative, when making requests.*** Not only do we need to be specific, we need to be positive. We usually get angry or defensive when someone makes a request of us in a negative way. People don't respond well to demands, ultimatums or criticism. So, instead of saying, "You never tell me about your day." Say, "I like it when you tell me about your day." Positive requests get results.

6. ***Remember to chose the right timing, setting and manner when you need to confront.*** Any way you look at it, confrontation is difficult. There's just no easy way to confront someone, especially your spouse. Yet, at times it is necessary for a husband or wife to confront the other about important issues. But make sure its really important. No relationship can endure a lot of confrontation. Be careful not to sound like a parent scolding a child when you confront

your partner. Keep the conversation on an adult-to-adult level characterized by calmness and objectivity. Positive growth can take place in your marriage when you confront the right way.

BEST FRIENDS

Here's the bottom line: Intimacy in marriage is based on the depth of open, honest, gut-level communication. No hidden agendas. No masks or defenses. No games of manipulation and control. When a husband and wife communicate this way, they become best friends. As C. Raymond Beran writes:

> Friends are people with whom you dare to be yourself. Your soul can be naked with them. They ask you to put on nothing, only to be what you are. They do not want you to be better or worse. When you are with them, you feel like a prisoner feels who has been declared innocent. You do not have to be on your guard. You can say what you think, as long as it is genuinely you. Friends understand those contradictions in your nature that lead others to misjudge you. With them, you breathe freely. You can avow your little vanities and envies and hates and vicious sparks, your meanness and absurdities, and in opening them up to friends, they are lost, dissolved on the white ocean of their loyalty. They understand. You do not have to be careful. You can abuse them, neglect them, and tolerate them. Best of all, you can keep still with them. It does not matter. They like you. They understand. You can weep with them, sing with them, laugh with them, pray with them. Through it all—and underneath— they see, know and love you. What is a friend? Just one, I repeat, with whom you dare to be yourself.[9]

CHAPTER FIVE

MAKING THE MOST OF YOUR MONEY

S OMEONE HAS APTLY STATED, "YOU WRITE YOUR AUTOBIOGRAPHY IN your checkbook." How we manage our money says a great deal about our moral values, personal priorities and individual character. Whether we like it or not money is intertwined in nearly every facet of our lives. Even Ecclesiastes says, *"Money is the answer for everything."*[1]

You may find it interesting to know that the Bible is filled with down-to-earth wisdom on financial management. While the Bible contains about 500 verses on faith and another 500 verses on prayer, it has over 2,000 verses on money. Also, 16 of Jesus' 38 recorded parables deal with the subject of money in one way or another.

When we boil it all down, sound financial management is based on three basic priorities: *give generously, save consistently and spend wisely.*

GIVE, GIVE, GIVE

There's a story about a man traveling through a blistering desert. He was faint with thirst and to his delight he came across a well with a pump. Next to the pump sat a small jug of water with a sign: "Please use this water to prime the pump. The well is deep, so you will have enough water for yourself and your containers. Please fill the jug for the next traveler."

What was he to do? Should he play it safe and drink the water in the jug, making sure that his parched thirst was quenched? Or, should he take the risk of pouring the water in the pump so both he could drink and he could provide for the next traveler in need?

Sound financial management begins with us deciding whether or not we will spend all we get to meet our own needs or whether we will share what we have with others. The greatest virtue of the Christian life is the spirit of giving. We are truly like God when we give: *"For God so loved the world that He gave His only begotten Son."*

Jesus said, *"Give, and it will be given to you. A good measure, pressed down, shaken together and running over, will be poured into your lap. For with the measure you use, it will be measured to you."* He also told us, *"It is more blessed to give than it is to receive."*[2]

Bob Pierce, founder of *World Vision* and *The Samaritan's Purse*, tells the story of a minister who received a letter of complaint from a wealthy, influential businessman in his church. The complaint came after the pastor had made an appeal for giving. The man wrote, "As far as I can see this Christian business is just one continuous give, give, give." The pastor wrote back a thank you note to the man. "I want to thank you for the best definition of the Christian life I have ever heard. As near as I can see you are correct: This Christian business, as you call it, is indeed just one continuous give, give, give."

I recall watching a financial planner on TV give a motivational talk on how to become independently wealthy. He shocked the audience when he said, "The first principle you need to learn if you want to be financially successful is to give away the first tenth of your income." It may have sounded revolutionary to his audience, but that's a biblical principle dating back to the time of Abraham, who lived about 2,000 years before the time of Christ. He gave a tenth of his wealth to God as an offering of praise. This principle is called *tithing*. (The word *tithe* means a tenth.)

Unfortunately, most people give far less than a tenth of their earned income. In fact, Americans on average only give about 3.7 percent of their income to charitable causes. What's even more interesting is that those who make the least give the most on a percentage basis. According to an 1998 Gallup poll, families with annual incomes under $10,000 gave 5.5 percent, while those in the $50,000-$60,000 bracket averaged only 1.7 percent! In addition, those in the $75,000-$99,999 bracket averaged 3.2 percent and those making $100,000 or more a year averaged only 2.9 percent. Another report I read recently revealed that if Americans increased their average giving by just one percent, it would generate an additional $62 billion for churches and humanitarian groups.

You may ask, why is giving so important?

First, we *acknowledge God's ownership of our possessions*. As I pointed out earlier, we do not actually own anything. Everything belongs to God. Since this is true, we need to see ourselves as managers of God's resources. We are responsible to manage the resources God gives us. This is why we print, "In God We Trust," on our currency — as a reminder that God owns it all and that He alone is our ultimate source of security.

Giving also *establishes eternal values and priorities in our lives*. Jesus said, *"For where your treasure is, there will your heart be also."* What a powerful statement. The way you manage your money has a great impact on the condition of your heart — that is your desires, aspirations, values and priorities. The inverse is also true — the condition of your heart determines how you will manage your money. You may not give your money away, but your money will give you away. Remember, you write your autobiography in your checkbook.

Let me encourage you to take time to review your last bank statement or the charges on your credit card. How are your spending your money? What do your purchases say about your spiritual life? As you review your expenses, notice both what is present in your financial statements and what is absent. Withholding our resources from those in need says as much about us as does frivolous spending. You can actually enhance your spiritual growth by giving. Giving enlarges the heart.

Giving also *keeps us from getting caught up in the love of money*. I'm sure you've heard the timeless biblical adage, *"The love of money is the root of all evil."* Notice that the verse doesn't say that money is the root of all evil but that the *love of* money is the root of all evil. A thought-provoking statement to say the least. Well, what is the love of money? The love of money is the all-consuming desire to get wealth at any cost. It is covetousness, envy and jealously over what others possess. It is the measurement of one's success by what he or she possesses. But, when we give freely, we break the hold that money has over us and find the meaning of true prosperity. The truly prosperous person doesn't measure her worth by what she has but by what she has given away.

Furthermore, giving is *an act of faith in God which frees us from the fear of poverty*. One wife shared with me in confidence one day that she believed her husband had a spirit of poverty. I found that to be an intriguing statement in view of the fact that they were very well off financially. You see, a person's level of financial success does not exempt him from the fear of poverty. In fact, sometimes the more money people make the more frightened they become that they might lose it all. They began to hoard their money in an effort to feel secure.

That's exactly what happened to young John D. Rockefeller, Sr. He was a determined businessman who set out to earn his fortune. By age 33 he earned his first million dollars. By 43 he controlled the largest company in the world. By 53 he was the richest man in the world and the world's only billionaire. He then developed a strange disease (alopecia) where his hair fell out, his eyebrows and eyelashes disappeared and he was shrunken like a mummy. While his weekly income was one million dollars, his diet consisted of milk and crackers. He was so hated in Pennsylvania that he maintained body guards. He couldn't sleep and all joy for living left him. The medical diagnosis predicted he would not live another year. The newspaper wrote his obituary in advance.

During those sleepless nights, he began to take stock of himself. He realized he could not take any of his money with him into the next world. One morning he awoke with new resolve. He began giving his money to hospitals, research and missions work. He helped the poor and needy. He established the Rockefeller Foundation whose funding led to the discovery of penicillin as well as cures for malaria, tuberculosis and diphtheria. He began to sleep again. Joy filled his heart. The symptoms began to disappear. Instead of dying at 54 as predicted he lived to be 98. Giving gave him new life!

Giving will also bring you success. A real estate agent by the name of Abner Bartlett arrived in Philadelphia with a few days off. Every major hotel turned him away — no rooms. All but one — the Bellevue. It only had 24 rooms all of which were full, the manager told Bartlett but added, "But, we can accommodate you." "I thought you were booked up," Bartlett responded. "We are. However, you and Mrs. Bartlett may have my private suite."

A few years later, his friend and client, William Waldorf Astor, consulted him about purchasing property to build a new five-star hotel in New York. Astor was skeptical about whether or not the hotel would make it financially, but Bartlett assured him the hotel would thrive in the section of town they selected. Astor said to Bartlett, "Do you have a man who can manage a hotel like that, if we decide to build it?" Bartlett replied firmly, "I know just the man."

George Boldt of the Bellevue became the first manager of the Waldorf Astoria.[3]

Now for the bottom line: Giving is an *act of worship to God.* Solomon wrote, *"Honor the Lord with your wealth, with the first fruits of all your crops; then your barns will be filled to overflowing and your vats will brim over with new wine."* As you evaluate your current financial status and future financial goals, make sure your strategy honors God. This is the most important key to financial success.

GET READY, THAT RAINY DAY IS COMIN'

As a nation we are beginning to save more than we have in the recent past, especially during the eighties. While the eighties was a decade of tremendous financial gains, those gains were not matched with responsible savings and investments. Americans were, by and large, on a big spending spree. Americans save only 2.5 percent of their income on average.

Saving money requires wisdom for sound financial investments. The story is told about John D. Rockefeller, Sr. who got into a taxi cab one day going to a meeting. The driver recognized him and asked if Rockefeller would give him some advice on how to invest a small amount of inheritance money he had received. Rockefeller told him, "You need to make wise decisions."

The cabby replied, "That's great advice, but tell me, how can I learn to make wise decisions?"

"You need experience."

"And how do I get experience?" the cabby asked.

Rockefeller said, "By making bad decisions."

If that be the case, I think it's safe to say we're all rich in experience. We have all made our share of bad decisions. Any way we look at it, we need to cultivate both the desire and discipline to save money if we ever hope to be financially secure. Saving pays great dividends in more than one way.

First of all, saving enables you to *build your own cash reserves.* Everybody needs cash reserves for unexpected expenses and emergencies. The problem is most of us borrow money from credit card institutions, a personal loan from family members or friends or a home-equity loan to handle emergencies. But when you consistently put your own money away, you build up your own cash reserves. You win on two counts: you avoid getting into debt and you earn interest on your savings instead of paying it to a lending institution. In other words, you become your own bank.

Saving also helps couples prepare for both *short-range and long-range financial goals* like taking a vacation, saving for the kid's college fund, making a down-payment on their first home or investing for retirement.

Maybe the most important benefit of saving is that it *curbs spending.* America is the number one consumer market in the world. While we represent only six percent of the world's population, we have about 90 percent of the world's advertising because we consume so many products. It takes a lot of self-discipline to avoid getting caught up in the American spirit of consumerism. Saving money will make you more conscientious about your spending habits. Since the money you save is out of reach, you'll be less likely to spend it impulsively.

Sounds great, how can I get started? you may ask. Here are a few tips to help as you begin:

1. *Liquidate consumer debt.* Pay off all credit cards and personal loans (excluding your home mortgage). The interest you pay each month eats away at your investment potential.

2. *Start small.* You may say, "I just don't have anything to put into savings." If you don't start now, even with a small amount, you may never get started. Saving money is a habit. It takes discipline. So break the bad habit of over-spending by starting your savings today.

3. *Be consistent.* Don't be hit-and-miss with your savings. Set a fixed amount in your budget and stick to it just as consistently as you pay your rent, mortgage or car payment.

4. *Eliminate waste.* Track your spending habits. Keep a log for a month and see where your money is going. Then make the necessary adjustments in your spending habits in order to free up some money for savings.

5. *Seek wise counsel regarding investment opportunities.* There are many excellent books and resources available to help you get started in planning your financial future. You may also want to consult a reputable financial planning agency to assist you. Whatever strategy you choose, get started today. Every day you wait means a loss of potential earnings on your investments.

HERE IT IS AND THERE IT GOES!

Now that we've discussed giving generously and saving consistently, let's talk about the greatest challenge of financial management — spending wisely. I heard about a Los Angeles economist who has written a new book entitled, *The Short Story of Money.* The book contains only seven words: "Here it is and there it goes."

Everyone needs to get a handle on spending money. Did you know that...

$ One-fifth of a person's income services his or her debts.

$ Forty percent of home equity loans are used to pay off other bills.

$ Americans are indebted up to 40 percent of their income.

$ Americans spend on average about 115 percent of income.[4]

$ During the nineties, gambling spending rose to about $330 billion per year from lotteries, casinos, tracks and so forth.

Some couples feel like they never have enough money. Consequently, they labor under a constant strain of financial stress living from hand to mouth. When conducting marriage seminars I often ask couples, "What is the number one source of stress in your marriage?" The most common response is financial stress. When you add it all up — paying bills, saving for the kid's college fund, retiring debt, paying exorbitant insurance rates, medical bills, investing for retirement and paying taxes — sometimes there's just not enough to go around.

It is important that couples learn to play to their strengths when it comes to managing their money. Olivia Mellan, a Washington, D.C. psychotherapist and author of *Overcoming Overspending,* gives some great advice on this point. She observes that people's personality types correlate with their attitudes toward money such as spenders, hoarders, worriers and avoiders. She goes on to point out that every type has both positives and negatives but in a successful relationship, spouses compliment one another.[5]

Tax truths. It has been pointed out that only two things are for certain in this life: death and taxes. Sometimes we aren't sure which one is worse. The average American works 34 percent of the year just to pay taxes. Arthur Godfrey said, "I feel honored to pay taxes in America. The thing is I could feel just as honored for about half the price."

April 15th represents financial D-Day for many. Tax day is in bad company among the all-time bad days in history. April 15th is also the day President Lincoln was assassinated and the day the *Titanic* sank! That about says it all. Jay Leno remarked, "President Clinton says he looks forward to the day a citizen can call the IRS and get the right answer to a question. I look forward to the day I can call the IRS and get a voice that says, 'Sorry, that number has been disconnected.'"

You may be interested in knowing just who pays what share of the total income tax burden. The top 25 percent of taxpayers, with annual incomes of $43,000 and more, account for 80 percent. The top 5 percent of taxpayers, with incomes of $91,000 and higher, pay

48 percent of income taxes. And the top 1 percent, with incomes of $196,000 and up, account for 29 percent of personal income taxes paid. Keep that in mind when you hear that upper-incomers don't pay enough.[6]

Are you an overspender? Effective money-management requires couples to learn to spend wisely. The first task is to determine whether or not you are an overspender. Overspenders share some common personality traits. To identify these, *Money* magazine asked 15 psychologists, credit counselors and financial planners to draw up this checklist. (Mark True or False and keep your score.)

1. *You spend money on the expectation that your income will rise.*
2. *You take cash advances on one credit card to pay off another.*
3. *You spend over 20 percent of your income on credit card bills.*
4. *You often fail to keep an accurate record of your purchases.*
5. *You have applied for more than five cards in the past year.*
6. *You regularly pay for groceries with a credit card because you need to.*
7. *You often hide your credit card purchases from your family.*
8. *Owning several credit cards makes you feel richer.*
9. *You pay off your monthly credit card bills but let others slide.*
10. *You like to collect cash from friends at restaurants, then charge the tab on your credit card.*
11. *You almost always make only the minimum payment on your credit card bill.*
12. *You have trouble imagining your life without credit.*

[Scoring: 1-4 true answers: You can probably keep going. You don't seem to splurge uncontrollably. 5-8 true answers: Slow down, you have entered the caution zone. It's time to draw up a budget, pay off bills and re-evaluate spending habits. 9-12 true answers: You must stop. It may be wise to consult a credit counselor or financial planner for help in changing your habits.][7]

How to live like a millionaire. Learning how millionaires live sheds some important light on developing healthy spending habits. Thomas J. Stanley spent twenty years studying how people become millionaires. During his years of research and writing three books on economics, he learned some invaluable lessons. First, there is a difference between income and wealth. If you make $500,000 a year and spend $500,000 a year, you're not getting wealthier you're just living too high. Wealth is what you accumulate not what you spend. In fact, most millionaires measure success by their net worth (the difference between your assets and your liabilities), not by their income.[8]

Most wealthy people keep their expenses under control. In one large metropolitan district he surveyed, less than half the millionaires lived in expensive sub-divisions. Instead of spending their money on expensive homes and luxury cars, they tend to invest their money for greater gains in other ventures. Here's an invaluable principle that will keep you in good stead financially — spend far less than you can afford for a home, cars, vacations and entertainment. Most millionaires pour their money into their businesses, stock portfolios and other assets instead of taking their money home and spending it.

Here's a profile of most American millionaires. The average person with a net worth of $1 million or more is a business person who has lived his or her adult life in the same town. He owns a small factory, chain of stores or a service company. Married once, and still married, he lives in a middle-class neighborhood. He saves and invests his money compulsively. And he's made it on his own: 80 percent are first-generation millionaires.

Consumer debt. Developing good spending habits also requires getting a handle on consumer debt. Seriously delinquent credit card debt already exceeds $4 billion in America as cards are used for everything from groceries to paying traffic fines. Non-card delinquencies are at record levels and still rising. Personal bankruptcies will top one million for the second straight year. Why is so much debt being amassed by American consumers? Mostly because of the increased leniency of bankruptcy laws and the fact that people get hooked on easy credit.

The average American household debt is now $11,600, not counting mortgages. And the debt is spread unevenly. Those with annual incomes of $50,000-$100,000 account for 60 percent of new debt and have added a lot in the past four years. Also there is a big increase in the share held by low-incomers, below $25,000, largely due to aggressive credit card promotions by banks, lending institutions and retailers. Individuals and families earning over $100,000 have a smaller share of debt than in 1992.[9]

Consumer debt is like a powder keg. One spark can set off an explosion leaving a family in financial ruin. So, before you incur a debt, take time to ask the following questions:

$ Can this new debt be avoided without disrupting our family?

$ Can this debt be avoided by some judicious short-term savings?

$ Will this debt severely strain our family's financial resources?

If you answer no to each, you are probably in a position to take on a limited debt for a specific purpose, provided you have a realistic plan for paying off the debt over a short period of time.[10]

Guidelines for spending. To avoid a financial catastrophe caused by credit spending, several guidelines need to be carefully followed:

1. *Evaluate your motives.* Financial advisor, Larry Burkett, says that before buying anything we should stop and ask ourselves, Is this purchase a need, a want or a desire? A *need* represents something we require for basic living like a car, or an appliance or health insurance. A *want* represents something we could use but could get

by without if we had to. A *desire* represents a pure indulgence, simply because we want it.

2. *Operate from a budget.* A budget requires us to review our spending on an annual, monthly, weekly and day-to-day basis. More will be said about how to develop a budget in a minute.

3. *Use a cash system.* Keep the use of credit cards to a minimum, especially if you have the tendency to delay paying off the balance every month. Some credit cards offer extra benefits like earning airfare miles or monthly refunds which provide advantages for using them. But if you can't control credit card expenses, or can't make the monthly payment in full, stick strictly to a cash system (including check-writing). This enables you to keep your spending current without being hit unexpectedly with large credit card balances each month. Many people fail to keep track of their credit card expenses and end up getting shocked when the bill comes due. WARNING! A couple has started down the hard road of escalating consumer debt when they use credit cards and make only the minimum payment.

4. *Be in agreement about expenditures.* How many marital arguments have resulted from one spouse spending money without first talking about it with their spouse? Such violations of "togetherness" breeds a lack of trust, disrespect and animosity. Spending money without being in agreement about those expenditures is an act of inconsideration, plain and simple. So talk about your expenditures before you make them. Such dialogue provides a check-and-balance system of financial accountability. You'll save more and spend more wisely in the long run if you do.

5. *Avoid consumer debt as much as possible.* When making a purchase ask, "How much does it cost?" instead of, "How much is the monthly payment?" The average family spends 13 percent of their annual income on consumer debt. Consumer debt refers to debt incurred on items that depreciate in value such as clothing, grocer-

ies or a vacation. Home mortgages, property purchases and financial investments are different from consumer debt because they typically increase in value over time.

6. *Try to spend only 80 percent of your net income.* Here's a simple rule to follow for financial success: Give 10 percent to charitable causes; save 10 percent; and use the other 80 percent for expenses. If you can give more and save more, by all means do. But this rule of 10/10/80 is a good place to start.

7. *Plan your spending.* Avoid impulsive and erratic purchases. Think it through before you make any purchase regardless of how large or small. Shop around for a better price, or at least better terms of payment if you have to purchase an item over a period of time.

8. *Expect the unexpected.* By doing so, you will automatically plan for emergencies. When couples obligate their total income to paying bills and retiring debt, they have a prescription for financial disaster. Sooner or later an emergency will arise, and they will lack the necessary funds to handle it. Without cash reserves of their own, they will have to borrow the money from an outside source. This, in turn, pushes their debt load over the desired limit. Now, the endless cycle of spiraling debt has started in their lives. Keep yourself free from debt by expecting the unexpected. Or, in the words of the old adage, save up for a rainy day. Or, maybe a flood!

9. *Keep you debt-load manageable.* Without a doubt, debt-free living is the ideal for which every couple should strive. But for many, that is the impossible dream right now. Debt can be used wisely to accomplish your goals. Before you purchase an item on credit, check to see if a merchant offers the item on 12-month, interest-free terms. If not, shop for the lowest possible interest terms. Then, pay off the debt as quickly as possible. A twelve-month payment plan is preferred over 36 months if you can handle the payments. Here's an important note: If you purchase an item for 12 months, interest-free, make sure you pay off the balance within the 12 month period.

If you are late, the entire accrued interest over that 12 month period comes due the next month. Many companies offer this deal because they know that most people do not have the discipline to pay off the balance within the 12-month period. So, the company ends up collecting the total interest amount.

10. *Distinguish between consumer debt and asset-accumulation debt.* The first house that Barbie and I built cost about $85,000. When we moved to another city eighteen months later, we sold it for $115,000. Six years later, a friend who still lived in that area told us that the house was on the market for $143,000. That's asset accumulation. Borrowing money to purchase a home can be an investment if done properly. There is always a risk involved, but the risk is minimal because real estate usually increases in value over time. An automobile, on the other hand, decreases in value over time. Debt incurred on a car constitutes consumer debt. The day you drive a new car off the lot it is worth considerably less than what you paid for it. (Unless you purchase a Rolls Royce!) Remember, consumer debt is an enemy to your long-range financial success. So eliminate it at all costs.

STOP FIGHTING ABOUT MONEY!

Share — don't argue about money. Financial pressure often results in sharp disagreements and unpleasant misunderstandings for couples. Elizabeth Razzi offers us some excellent tips on diffusing money disputes:

- Talk with each other about money openly and matter-of-factly. Silence could lead to unpleasant surprises.

- Add up your debts and devise a plan to pay them off.

- Settle the issue of joint-versus-separate accounts. Either will work if you both accept it. Or you could both chip in to fund a third kitty for the household.

- Designate who will pay the bills, balance the checkbook and handle investments. Whether you pool your money or keep separate accounts, someone has to do the financial house-keeping.

- Know where you money is. Even if your spouse is the numbers whiz, you need to touch base so you know how much is in the checking account and how much you owe on your credit cards.

- Don't begrudge your spouse's small indulgences. Each of you should have discretionary money to spend.

- Consult on large purchases.

- Don't criticize your spouse about money in front of others.

- Coordinate your responses when your kids ask for something, so they don't play one parent against the other.

- Discuss your goals regularly, preferably when you're not under the gun to solve a money problem. Even when you keep separate accounts, you need to coordinate financial plans — if you hope to retire *together.* [11]

THE BIG BAD "B" WORD

The only way to turn your financial dreams into reality is to develop a budget. Even Congress has gotten on board talking about the benefits of a balanced budget. A budget is simply a tool to help balance the "cash flow," that is, the flow of money as it comes in (income) and as it goes out (expenditures). Good record-keeping along with the close scrutiny of the budget gives a couple tremendous control over their money.

Here's how you can get started: Write out an annual budget first and then break it down into a monthly budget. Follow these guidelines as you prepare your budget:

$ The budget needs to be *written* not just discussed verbally.

$ The budget needs to be *realistic* reflecting both net income and projected expenditures.

$ The budget needs to be *agreed upon* by all parties involved.

$ The budget needs to be *balanced* into four categories: *charitable giving, living expenses, debt- reduction* and *savings* (both short-term and long-term). A budget is balanced in several ways. First, a budget is balanced when your expenses do not exceed income. Which means don't borrow from Peter to pay Paul. Also, money allocated for certain expenses needs to be used strictly for those purposes. For example, don't use living expenses to paying off debts early (unless, of course, such a shift of funds could be made without limiting the funds needed for family expenses). Or, don't use money allocated for savings for an impulsive vacation if the funds are allocated for your cash reserves. Think of your budget as a pie divided into these four categories and keep your money in its designated area. Any shifting of funds between the categories needs to be kept to a minimum once the budget is established. This will keep your budget in balance.

$ The budget needs to be *reviewed, updated and modified* periodically. Since a family's needs and obligations change from time to time, the budget needs to be updated, at least at the beginning of each new year. Remember to make your budget firm enough to keep you on track with your financial goals, yet flexible enough to accommodate changes that occur in your lifestyle.

Let me share a few simple tips on setting up a budget if you haven't done one before or if you want to revise your current budget.

1. Design a budget based on net monthly income and average monthly expenditures. Use the actual dollar amounts not hypothetical figures.

2. Include *all* fixed expenditures in your budget. Be careful to not omit any expenses even if you have to average certain costs such as groceries, clothing or medical expenses.

3. Distinguish between fixed and flexible expenditures. An example of a fixed expense is your rent, or mortgage or car payment. These monthly payments are fixed; there's no negotiation with the creditor each month concerning how much you owe. On the other hand, entertainment or clothing is a flexible expenditure. This means you have control over the amount your spend. You can go out on a $50 date or a $200 date, depending on where you go and what you do. You can purchase a $250 suit or a $1000 suit. You see, you control how much you spend on these items. You need to pay for these flexible expenses out of your monthly surplus after you have met all your fixed expenses.

4. Use your monthly surplus — what's left over after paying the bills and making investments — to determine you flexible expenditures.

5. Pay yourself first! Make sure you use your money to secure your own financial future by investing in your retirement plan or personal savings. You'll enjoy managing more if you pay yourself first. What a tragedy when couples are strapped financially to the point that they don't have any "fun money," for dates, small indulgences or vacations.

First Things First

Perhaps the most important principle to remember in getting your financial house in order is to establish and maintain financial priorities — priorities that govern your giving, your savings and investments and your spending. And, stick to your priorities even in tough times. This way, you'll be sure to reach your goals.

While the Titanic was sinking into the freezing, raging waters of the North Atlantic, a frightened woman in a lifeboat, about to be lowered into the water suddenly remembered something she needed which was in her room. She asked permission to go back to her room. She was given three minutes or they would leave without her. She ran across the deck that was already slanted at a dangerous angle. Racing through the gambling room with all the money rolled to one side, ankle deep, she came to her stateroom and quickly pushed aside her diamond rings, bracelets and necklaces as she reached to the shelf above her bed and grabbed three small oranges. She then rushed back to the lifeboat and got in.

What is incredible about her actions is that 30 minutes earlier, before the ship hit an iceberg she would have never chosen three oranges over her priceless jewelry. But death had boarded the Titanic and transformed all sense of values. The priceless became worthless and the worthless became priceless.

When handling money, we need to keep our sense of what is really valuable in life. Remember the words of Jesus when it comes to setting financial priorities, *"Seek first the kingdom of God and His righteousness and all these things will be given to you as well."*

CHAPTER SIX

LOVING YOUR WAY TO BETTER SEX

HAVE YOU EVER HEARD THE STORY ABOUT THE ANT AND THE elephant? They were childhood sweethearts. They loved each other so much that they wanted to spend the rest of their lives together. On their wedding night they discovered that sex was incredible. Neither the ant nor the elephant had ever experienced such pleasure. The next morning the ant woke up and, to its horror, discovered the elephant dead. Heartbroken, the ant looked up to heaven and moaned, "Woe is me! Just one night of ecstasy and now I have to spend the rest of my life digging a grave."

That about sums up the state of affairs for many couples when it comes to their sex life. Research indicates that at least 50 percent of all marriages are flawed by some form of sexual difficulty or dysfunction. Many couples find themselves trapped in an endless cycle of sexual problems and marital unhappiness that feed off each other.[1]

Today it seems like you don't read a lot about sex getting better for married couples. I heard that scientists have recently discovered a food that greatly reduces sex drive — it's called a wedding cake.

Let's set the record straight right up front: Happily married couples enjoy good sex. Anyone who suggests that sex isn't that important in marriage just isn't shooting straight with you. (Or, they're not married.) True, sex is more important for some couples than it is for others. But the joyful sharing of sexual love is a key factor in the marriage equation.

The Bible celebrates the joy of sex: *"May your fountain be blessed, and may you rejoice in the wife of your youth. A loving doe, a graceful deer—may her breasts satisfy you always, may you ever be captivated by her love."* Some of the most erotic and seductive language in all literature appears in the Song of Solomon. In this magnificent song, which celebrates the joys of sexual love, the bride says to her bridegroom, *"Place me like a seal over your heart, like a seal on your arm; for love is as strong as death, its jealousy unyielding as the grave. It burns like blazing fire, like a mighty flame. Many waters cannot quench love; rivers cannot wash it away. If one were to give all the wealth of his house for love, it would be utterly scorned."*[2]

One study showed that 60 percent of the wives who rated their marriages as very happy reached orgasm 90 to 100 percent of the time during intercourse. Thirty-eight percent of the wives who rated their marriages as very unhappy never or rarely reached orgasm (only 1 to 9 percent of the time) during intercourse. These findings suggest a positive correlation between marital happiness and sexual orgasm. However, the same study also showed that 4 percent of the wives who rated their marriage as very happy never had orgasms, and that 38 percent of the wives who rated their marriages as very unhappy practically always had orgasms.

All this simply means that good sex isn't the cure-all for all marital problems, neither does it guarantee a happy marriage. Nevertheless, according to the study, it was harder for wives to be happily married without orgasm, and it was harder to have an orgasm without a happy marriage.[3]

The point is, good sex and a good marriage go hand in hand. Married couples need both a commitment to their marriage covenant and a commitment to the development of their sexual relationship. We are in need of a new definition of marital faithfulness in our day. I mean, the concept of faithfulness is so narrowly defined in such negative terms to only mean a person who has not had sexual intercourse outside marriage. But there is more to faithfulness than that.

Andrew Greenly points out that faithfulness — which is part of every human relationship — is "the striving toward permanence, a longing for a love that does not end. It is the permanent commitment to 'reach out' for the other person, a promise to persist in efforts to transcend the distance between, a firm resolve to sustain the relationship, no matter what difficulties arise."[4]

It is unlikely for married lovers to develop such faithfulness unless they have a strong commitment to increasing their enjoyment in sex. This begins with understanding the world of sexual pleasure and, in particular, the needs of one's partner. Let's be honest: No one is born with all the refined skills for lovemaking. These are only acquired through experience, trial and error, through the ability to learn from failures and from getting feedback from your partner. Every lover needs to be told what he or she is doing right and what wrong, and always in a positive way.

So, developing sexual intimacy begins with learning the basics of lovemaking. I think you'll enjoy this story. I heard about a minister who was asked to give a talk at a local women's health symposium. His wife asked about his topic, but he was too embarrassed to admit that he had been asked to speak about sex. Thinking quickly, he replied, "I'm talking about sailing."

"Oh, that's nice," his wife said. The next day at the grocery store, a young woman who had attended the lecture recognized the minister's wife. "That was certainly an excellent talk your husband gave yesterday," she said. "He really has a unique perspective on the subject."

Somewhat chagrined, the minister's wife replied, "Gee, funny you should think so. I mean, he's only done it twice. The first time he threw up and the second time, his hat blew off."

IN SEARCH OF INTIMACY

It has been said that love is "a many-splendored thing." Well, so is lovemaking. For starters, sex involves romance. This is the adventurous, charming, erotic and passionate side of love. Romance brings patience, gentleness, arousal, excitement and love-talk into the act of love. Leo Buscaglia gives some insightful tips for cultivating romance:

1. Tell me often that you love me, through your talk, your actions and your gestures. Don't assume that I know it, I may show signs of embarrassment and even deny that I need it — but don't believe me. Do it anyway.
2. Compliment me often for jobs well done, and don't downgrade but reassure me when I fail. Don't take the many things I do for you for granted.
3. Let me know when you feel low or lonely or misunderstood. It will make me stronger to know that I have the power to comfort you. Remember, though I love you, I still can't always read your mind.
4. Express joyous thoughts and feelings. They bring vitality to our relationship.
5. Don't invalidate me by telling me what I see or feel is insignificant or not real. It's my experience and therefore important and real!
6. Listen to me without judgment or preconception.
7. Let others know you value me. Public affirmation of our love makes me feel special and proud. [5]

I was conducting a premarital counseling session with a young couple and we were talking about the importance of continuing "the chase" even after they got married. The groom to be said, "I know exactly what you mean." He turned to his fiancé and said, "After we get married, I still want to be your boyfriend." Let me tell you, that guy understood the meaning of romance. But so many couples stop pursuing each other. The chase suddenly ends when they say, "I do." So make sure that you don't allow sex to become commonplace in your marriage. Keep the romance alive.

Sex also involves a powerful exchange of emotional energy between lovers. Positive feelings of security, significance, self-worth, belongingness and being loved and needed are generated when couples make love. However, such negative feelings of fear, low self-esteem, inadequacy and depression can also come into play. When a husband and wife share themselves sexually, they unite their personalities, moods and temperaments. When they do it can either be like a Fourth of July celebration with fireworks or like World War III depending on how they blend together. My point is, sex is more than merely a physical experience resulting in ten seconds of ecstatic pleasure called orgasm. Sexual love unites two unique personalities together as one in the bond of true intimacy.

ASK AND YOU SHALL RECEIVE

While learning about sexuality from a general standpoint is helpful, it is not nearly as important as understanding the specific needs of your spouse. Generalizations and stereotypes about men and women can lead to serious misunderstandings between a husband and wife.

I was reading an article recently in which a newly-wed husband said that his wife was acting a certain way when they made love, and it really turned him off. Finally, he mustered up the courage to say something to her about it. She was shocked that her behavior in bed was such a turn off. "Why do you act that way?" he asked her. She said, "I've always heard that that's what men like sexually so I was doing it because I thought that's what you wanted." She was relieved when he told her she didn't have to act that way because she didn't like it either. You see, she was simply doing what she thought her husband would enjoy, but never asked him directly.

It is important that husbands and wives talk openly to each other about their sexual needs and desires. And don't expect your partner to read your mind. Sex starts with talking not touching. The simple rule of good journalism can help on this point. Ask, Who? What? When? Where? and How? Here are some examples:

✓ *Who usually initiates making love?*
✓ *At what time of day do you usually make love?*
✓ *Do you like to make love in the morning, afternoon or evening?*
✓ *What I like most about our sex life is ...*
✓ *What can I do to make sex more satisfying for you?*
✓ *What I would like more of in our sexual relationship is...*
✓ *What are the conditions that put you in the mood?*
✓ *How often do you like to make love?*
✓ *Where do you enjoy making love?*
✓ *What is the easiest way for you to achieve orgasm?*
✓ *What are your sexual inhibitions?*
✓ *What makes you self-conscious or embarrassed?*
✓ *My favorite sexual fantasy about you is...*

These are the kinds of issues and experiences couples need to talk about. Remember, good sex starts with open communication. When is the last time you and your partner talked openly about your sex life? Let me encourage you to take some time to do so.

WHAT PLANET ARE YOU FROM?

Author John Gray says that men are from Mars and women are from Venus. When it comes to sex, it's obvious that we are from different planets. Much has been written about the sexual differences between men and women. It reminds me of the story I heard about a man who was walking on the beach one day and found a bottle. He didn't see anyone around so he opened the bottle. Suddenly, a genie appeared. "Thanks for letting me out of that bottle," said the genie. "I will grant you one wish. But I can only grant one."

The man said, "I've always wanted to go to Hawaii. I've never been able to go because I cannot fly. Airplanes are much too frightening for me. On a boat, I see all that water and I become very claustrophobic. So I wish for a road to be built from here to Hawaii."

The genie thought for a minute then replied, "No, I can't do that. Just think of all the work involved. Consider all the pilings needed to hold up a highway and how deep they would have to go to reach the bottom of the ocean. Imagine all the pavement needed. No, that is just too much to ask. You'll have to make another wish."

So, the man said, "Well, there is something else I've always wanted. I would like to be able to understand women. What makes them laugh and cry, why they are temperamental, why they are so difficult to get along with. Basically, what makes them tick."

Pausing for a moment, the genie said, "So, tell me, do you want two lanes or four?"

What we share in common. Before we delve any further into our differences, let's talk about some things we share in common. While men and women do have some basic differences in their sexual preferences, they aren't as far apart as you might think. As Philip Rice, in *Sexual Problems In Marriage*, points out:

> Differences that exist are largely the result of cultural conditioning. Women are still reared to believe that it is only right to give themselves sexually to the man they love, whereas men are still reared to try to prove their manhood through sexual prowess, and to prove their...masculinity. As a consequence, men and women do express their sexuality some-

what differently. However, most men have just as great a need for closeness, tenderness, real concern, sympathetic understanding, and affection as do women. They have been taught to suppress their feelings, but the needs are still there. Why else are so many men attracted to warm, maternal, tender, and understanding women? It is my firm conviction that men want their deepest emotional needs fulfilled in their sexual relationships. When these needs are not satisfied, men do feel that something is lacking.

At the same time, modern research has revealed that not only do women want love and affection but that they also want sex: beautifully erotic, wonderfully pleasurable and uninhibited sex, and that after generations of repression they have discovered their sexuality and found they can enjoy sex as much as man. Many women have even a greater capacity than men have. They are often multi-orgasmic, inhibitions are broken down and women can love sex as much as they desire love, just as a man can love as much as he wants sex.

The task of the couple, therefore, is to cultivate love, and then to learn to use the body as a means of expressing inner feelings, emotions and sexual urges. In this sense, sex has a spiritual function, to be a physical means of expressing an inward grace. When sex is lifted above the level of just physical expression and response, it becomes most satisfying to human beings.[6]

Mastering the art of lovemaking begins with a basic understanding of the sexual uniqueness of men and women. Richard Restak points out that, "Recent psychological research indicates that many of the differences in brain function between the sexes are innate, biologically determined and relatively resistant to change through the influences of culture."[7] He goes on to cite David Wechsler, creator of perhaps the most popular intelligence test for use with adults: "Our findings do confirm what poets and novelists have often asserted and the average layman long believed, namely, that men not only behave but 'think' differently from women."[8]

Getting turned on. Sexual arousal differs in some respects between men and women. Men are aroused primarily by visual stimulation while women are aroused more by touching and talking. Women are also more discriminating in their sexual interests. James Dobson once remarked, "If I had the power to communicate only one message to every family in America, I would specify the importance of romantic love to every aspect of feminine existence. It provides the foundation for a woman's self-esteem, her joy in living and her sexual responsiveness."[9]

Keep in mind that kissing is a deeply intimate expression of sexual love for both men and women. Not only does kissing bring intense physical pleasure, it also demonstrates a sense of intimacy, care and respect. So, cultivate the art of sensual kissing. Also, remember that sexual arousal comes from both touching and seeing. So the way you dress, or undress, can be as stimulating to your partner as how you touch and caress each other.

Maybe it goes without saying, but let's say it anyway: Good health is vital to good sex. So take care of yourself physically. It shows that you respect both yourself and your partner. Personal hygiene, weight-control, proper exercise and nutritious eating are all part of the plan for a great sex life together.

Achieving orgasm. Over the past few decades women have been taught that they can and should have orgasms as easily as men — even easier because they have the capacity for multiple orgasms which men lack. Despite all this training, the fact remains that many women have more difficulty than men in achieving orgasm during intercourse. One study shows that only 41.5 percent of women regularly experience orgasm during intercourse alone, without additional stimulation. Instead, 33 percent of women choose to experience orgasm during foreplay and a smaller percentage after intercourse.[10]

Why *don't* the majority of women achieve orgasm during intercourse? No one knows for sure, but one thing is certain: women have a higher threshold of orgasmic response than men. Which simply means that it takes more effort and concentration for them to achieve orgasm. It is unfortunate that many women feel sexually inadequate if they don't regularly have orgasms because they have been taught that if they relaxed more, or learned different techniques, then they could become as orgasmic as men.

Every husband needs to understand a very important aspect of feminine sexuality: women can and usually do enjoy sex with or without orgasm. So, if orgasm is not the ultimate goal of intercourse for many women, what is? Their first goal is what is termed "a state of arousal." Professor Uta Landy, from the University of California, says, "Physiologically, arousal seems to be a pulsing, a push, a throbbing throughout the entire pelvic region which means a readiness for intercourse. The feeling is spread much wider throughout the body than it is in men, where it is usually concentrated in the sex organ." For some women, it is a pleasant, "tingly" feeling; for others it is ecstatic.[11] For many women, arousal is not the pathway to orgasm, it is a goal in itself resulting in a great sense of sexual satisfaction.

Landy goes on to point out that arousal is not only physically satisfying, it also generates feelings of affection and closeness. These feelings are heightened by intromission — the feeling of the male inside her — which constitutes an important part of sex for women even though it may not lead to orgasm. Studies show that most women do not feel that sex is complete without intercourse. Even when women did not expect to achieve a climax, nearly all of them desired intercourse anyway. This suggests that intercourse has a meaning all its own for women, apart from achieving orgasm.[12] So, it is not only orgasm that counts with women — it is arousal that brings them a sense of emotional as well as physical pleasure.

Romance or recreation? While women cherish romance, men tend to enjoy sex as a form of what we might call recreational love. So, who's right? Well, there's plenty of room for diversity in a couple's sexual relationship. Wives should learn to enjoy sex as pure physical pleasure as well as being romantic, and husbands need to cultivate the fine art of romantic love, not just "cutting to the chase." When they do it's a win-win proposition for both parties.

We need to set the record straight on one crucial point concerning the sexual differences between men and women. Men have gotten a bad rap when it comes to giving and receiving sexual pleasure. Contrary to popular opinion, men do not simply look out for number one when it comes to making love. In fact, a husband finds great satisfaction in giving his wife pleasure. Men tend to pride themselves when they know they have pleased their wives sexually. It's easy for a man to get pleasure for himself while making love. That doesn't require any skill. The art lies in giving his wife sexual pleasure. When he does, he feels good about himself. Every husband who truly loves his wife with covenant love will put her needs for sexual satisfaction ahead of his own.

While some women complain that all their husband wants from them is sex, they fail to realize that sex is a way that a husband expresses his love to and for his wife. So, instead of resisting his advances, a wife is better off responding openly to his advances and enjoy God's gift of lovemaking. A smart wife will go out of her way to seduce her husband. And a smart husband will go to any extreme necessary to give his wife the romance she likes.

SEX SECRETS FOR HUSBANDS

Kathleen McCoy offers some excellent insights for husbands and wives to help them understand their sexual needs and desires. Here are the five most frequently cited "sex secrets" wives wish their husbands knew:[13]

1. *Great sex — for a woman — begins with her life as a whole.* Most women need positive feelings throughout the day and about their marriage in general to have satisfying sex. How a husband treats his wife out of bed greatly influences her responsiveness in bed.

2. *Many women find talk a turn-on.* Good conversations over dinner can be an aphrodisiac. Tender words during love-making, such as a man telling his wife how much he loves her, increases a woman's desire. For many women, talking and feeling loved are more important than sex.

3. *Women, too, have performance anxiety.* Many women feel pressure to have orgasms, when their primary goal is to simply be with the one they love.

4. *Warm attention after sex can be vital to a woman's satisfaction.* This is not always the case, but many women find the tender moments after actual lovemaking to be most satisfying.

5. *Women need nonsexual touching and tenderness.* Women want romance, cuddling, holding hands and kissing in as well as out of bed. Most importantly, a husband needs to tell his wife often, "I love you."

SEX SECRETS FOR WIVES

Here are the top five sex secrets men wish their wives knew, according to McCoy's research:[14]

1. *Men do not have a greater sex drive than women do.* Some men have a high level of sexual desire, others have very little — and the same is true for women. Age and lifestyle certainly affect a man's sex drive which means that married couples have to communicate about their sex life to avoid any confusion about what they both want sexually.

2. *Men do not want "just one thing."* The mature man will not seek to prove himself through sexual performance but will de-

sire communication on a variety of levels. And men want romance, affection and intimacy as much as women do.

3. *Love is an important factor in male sexual pleasure.* While not all agree, many say that love makes a crucial difference in sexual fulfillment. Men tend to be like women in that the more emotionally involved they are, the more intense their physical satisfaction.

4. *Men need foreplay too.* While men want to feel pampered and loved, to be touched and kissed, many find it difficult to ask for this. But they do enjoy it.

5. *Men do not always want to initiate sex.* Most men are excited by a woman's loving, tender assertiveness in bed. Her sexual initiative makes a man feel more desirable and relieved of the sole responsibility for sexual overtures.

SETTING BOUNDARIES

Often couples, especially those with a strong spiritual relationship, are concerned about the boundaries of sexual freedom in marriage. That may sound strange to you, but stop and consider the fact that everyone has certain values and beliefs about sexuality that govern their behavior. Sometimes we are aware of these values and beliefs but often we are guided by them without knowing it. Consequently, persons may be inhibited by performing certain sexual acts or even feel guilty because of their beliefs. I think three primary questions need to be answered about particular sexual acts to help couples set their own boundaries:

First, is it moral? Obviously, from a biblical perspective if Scripture identifies certain behaviors as immoral, couples should refrain from engaging in them.

Second, is it mutually satisfying? Whatever couples do sexually should be mutually satisfying to both of them. No person should be coerced into performing sexual acts with which he or she is uncomfortable. Perhaps the most controversial issue in setting boundaries concerns oral sex. Ed and Gay Wheat offer wise counsel on this point: "Oral sex...is a matter which concerns only the husband and wife involved. If both of you enjoy it and find it pleasant, then it may properly fit into your lovemaking practices. If either partner has any hesitancy about it, however, it will add little to the pleasure of the relationship and should be discontinued."[15]

Third, is it meaningful? Sexual love reaches its highest expression when couples achieve greater closeness, trust and intimacy as a result of making love. Sexual love is a pathway to a greater goal: the union of two lives into one.

PRACTICE MAKES PERFECT

True, as a couple grows together through the seasons of life, their sexual relationship changes. As they move into their forties and beyond, the rules for lovemaking change. The good news is sex can get better with age, if you know how it's done. No couple is too old to enjoy the inexplicable pleasures of lovemaking. Sex can be for better *not* worse.

It's like the elderly couple I heard about who got into bed one night. The man had just about dozed off to sleep when his wife whispered in his ear, "Honey, you use to hold my hand when we got into bed." So he reached over, held her hand and proceeded to go to sleep.

Then she said, "You use to cuddle up with me when we got into bed." A little agitated by this time, he rolled over and put his arms around her thinking that would surely satisfy her.

He started to doze off again until she whispered, "Honey, you use to nibble on my ears when we got into bed." With that he threw back the covers, jumped out of bed and started across the room.

"What's wrong?" she pleaded. "Where are you going?"

He said, "I'm going to get my teeth!"

The moral of the story is—keep the romance alive! Even if you have to get your teeth.

Here are a few tips to help you keep the fire burning as the years roll on. After all, staying in love is just as important as falling in love.

First, as couples get older, *the nature of romance changes.* Romance moves from being that you can't keep your hands off each other feeling, to the reassuring knowledge that you are loved by someone who really knows you and loves you just like you are. The old adage is often true, "Familiarity breeds contempt." But familiarity also has a positive side — it brings the joy of security. You learn to trust someone with whom you have come to share the totality of yourself in a deeply secretive and intimate relationship where the whole world is shut out. Over the years, you build a history of dreams fulfilled, tragedies endured and joys experienced that brings a sense of safety about each other. The heart and soul of real intimacy is a knowledge of each other, and that takes years to achieve.

Couples also have to *accept the reality of hormonal changes* as the years pass. Whether we like it or not, certain physiological, psychological and lifestyle changes brought on by middle-age have a profound effect on sexual drive and sexual needs. Women have to deal with menopause, the average age of which is the early fifties, which is brought on by a decrease in female hormones. As men get older, they experience a decrease in testosterone which, in turn, affects their desire for sexual love. These changes, however, do not have to diminish the quality of a couple's love life.

After forty, you may have to *alter the pace of lovemaking.* Men move beyond the fast, overly-aggressive sexual pace of their twenties and thirties and begin to slow down. Which simply means that most men don't want or need to have sex as often as they did when they first got married. If your husband is slowing down, it doesn't mean he doesn't love you any more. It just means he is getting older. After all, men hit their sexual prime around 17 and it continues until they are about 30. It's normal for them to slow down after 30.

It also helps to *take turns taking the lead*. It is not uncommon for men to become less aggressive and to initiate sex less frequently as they get older. So, wives need to initiate lovemaking more as the relationship matures. Most men enjoy their wives taking the lead some of the time and are not at all intimidated by their advances.

Remember to be *innovative.* Try new ideas or even revisit some old ones like going parking. That's not to say that you have to turn your sex life into a laboratory experiment, as some sex manuals imply. But variety is the spice of life. So, vary your sexual encounters from mornings to evenings, from planned liaisons to spontaneous "quickies." (I hope I'm not getting too specific here, but it's easier to write this in a way that you get the point. Otherwise the information is useless.)

Finally, as couples get older, they learn to *receive more from less.* While sexual experiences may be less frequent for older couples than their younger counterparts, they can be more meaningful. Over the years a couple learns to master the delicate art of bringing each other deeply satisfying sexual pleasure. After all, practice makes perfect.

JUMPING THE HURDLES

I wish I could omit this section but many couples face a host of hurdles that hinder sexual intimacy. Sometimes it's nothing more than simply not knowing what one's partner needs. Other times it is something more serious and complex. That's why it is vital that couples talk about their sex life. I can't underscore this point too much. Good communication is the core of sexual fulfillment.

Let's take a look at some common sexual problems couples face and some workable solutions. Sexual problems can stem from *stress, fatigue and the loss of quality time* for sexual pleasure. When the kids come along couples find themselves driven by an endless list of things to do and places to go. By the time they get home in the evening after working, fixing dinner, helping the kids with their homework and getting them in bed, the last thing on their minds is making love. Sleep, not sex, is number one! Sometimes boredom sets in. Routine replaces romance. When this happens reignite your sexual passion. Get out of the routine. Change your surroundings if you have to. Go off on a weekend together to a cozy Bed and Breakfast. Plan a candlelight dinner and surprise your husband, or your wife, when he or she arrives home.

Another less common area of sexual difficulty concerns *issues of the past* such as sexual abuse in childhood, premarital sexual trauma or sexual problems in a previous marriage. Repressed guilt about past sexual encounters, struggles with pornography, shame about an abortion, the fear of pregnancy and raising children, the fear of rejection, impotency and feelings of inadequacy can keep a couple from reaching their sexual potential together. Counseling needs to be sought to deal with these kinds of serious and often deep-seated issues.

When couples aren't getting along, or their *emotional needs are going unmet* in the relationship, sex turns sour fast. Marital dissatisfaction and sexual problems combine to form an endless cycle of hurt, anger and depression. Sex can be used as manipulation in a marriage. Withholding sex or demanding it are ways in which some partners assert their authority and get favors or decisions from each other. Sometimes the power plays are discussed openly. But more often sexual manipulation is expressed passively. The person who says, "I'm too tired to make love," or "I don't feel very well," may actually mean, "I'm going to get even with you by withholding my love," or "I'll get my way by controlling our sex life."

Sexual problems can also result from *biological and psychological causes.* Endocrine disturbances, obesity, low-energy levels and various physical problems can wreak havoc on a couple's sex life.

Then, there are emotional factors that come into play such as depression, fear, inadequacy. Feelings are easily hurt. Egos are wounded. Fears arise. Couples confront a whole host of emotional issues that can keep them from achieving sexual fulfillment ranging from feelings of insecurity and a sense of embarrassment to thoughts of inadequacy.

The worst sexual problem that can occur in a couple's life is *an affair.* Research indicates that the three primary causes of affairs are loneliness, monotony and the failure to communicate.[16] In our day of lowered sexual standards, which not only overlook but even condone extra-marital affairs, couples need to affair-proof their marriages. Temptations abound and opportunities for unfaithfulness are plenteous. Couples can affair-proof their marriage by spending time together, keeping the communication lines open and stoking the fires of their romance.

If you are experiencing difficulties in your sexual life, don't pretend that the problem will go away by itself. It won't. You need to address the problem head-on. Seek counseling together or see your physician. Sexual love is too important in your marriage for you to allow any problem to go unchecked.

EIGHT WAYS TO IMPROVE YOUR SEX LIFE

Let's put everything we've discussed into a workable plan of action. Here are eight steps to improve your sex life together:

1. *Make sex a priority.* All couples, regardless of their age, need to make sex a priority in their relationship. Remember to keep a balance between the romantic times and just having fun. Be generous with compliments and love-talk. Break the routine. Try new things together. And go out on dates.

2. *Be a hopeless romantic.* Remember the adage, "sex starts in the kitchen." I once read that sex starts when your clothes are still on. So, what do you need to be a romantic?

✓ The thoughtful card. The affectionate touch. The unexpected gift.

✓ The surprise phone call: "I just thought I'd call and tell you that I was thinking about you and can't wait till you get home." (Ladies, this one will insure you that he'll be home from work early!)

✓ The spoken word: "Have I told you lately how much I love you?"

✓ The unexpected compliment: "You know, honey, you are the most beautiful woman in the world to me."

✓ The inviting, reassuring touch at dinner.

These can all add up to wonderful evenings together.

3. *Tell your partner what you want.* Don't be embarrassed or hesitant to talk specifically to your partner about what you enjoy sexually. But choose your words carefully when you do. Always be positive. Open communication is the surest key to good sex.

4. *Spend a lot of time together.* The problem is that couples have too much TV and not enough time. The average American adult watches about 24 hours of television every week. Many couples get into the habit of turning on the television to relax when they get into bed. Yet, studies show that TV doesn't help us relax at all. In fact, according to The Annenberg School of Communications, too much television viewing contributes to people's feelings of anxiety and mistrust. Television keeps a couple from meaningful interaction. It becomes a substitute for intimacy. So turn off the television and turn on each other.

5. *Assume responsibility for your own sexual pleasure.* While men seem more comfortable with this idea, many women have been conditioned culturally to be far too passive in lovemaking. Women who think of themselves as merely responders to their husbands' sexual initiatives will often fail to achieve their full sexual potential.

This means that a wife must openly share her feelings and needs with her husband. She also needs to take the lead on occasion and during lovemaking to "show him how" to bring her pleasure.

6. ***Don't let the sun go down while you are still angry.*** Unresolved conflicts ruin more potentially romantic evenings than anything else. Maybe you need to get a poster from the 70's that says, "Make love — not war!" and put it in your bedroom. That's good advice for couples. Make sure you empty your anger storage tank before getting in bed by talking through your issues together. Here's my advice: *Get out* what you feel so you can *get over it* and then you can *get on* with living and loving. Write it down if you need to: Get it out. Get over it. Get on with it.

7. ***Don't be overly sensitive.*** Share—don't argue—about sex. Don't take every negative sexual encounter so personally. Every couple has those times when the romantic evening planned bombs out. Just forget about those times without blaming each other for the fiasco. Try to laugh about it together. Remember not to take yourself too seriously.

8. ***Maintain the sense of mystery.*** Over the years, this is harder to do because a husband and wife know each other so well and they have shared about every kind of sexual experience possible. So, how does a couple keep sex from becoming routine? Well, to begin with, there is no substitute for the unexpected surprise. Maybe it's just dinner together at the spur of the moment, or a phone call in the middle of the day to say, "I love you," or having your husband come home to a candlelight dinner and the finest negligée. Whatever it takes, keep your love fresh and exciting.

Finally, above everything else, let go of your inhibitions and enjoy the private world of sexual joy God has given you to explore and share together.

CHAPTER SEVEN

THE MISSING LINK

T HE GERMAN AGNOSTIC, NIETZCHE, BOASTED, "GOD IS DEAD." WHEN
I think of his assertion, I'm reminded of a New York City
subway where someone spray-painted graffiti on the wall
the words, "God is dead," and underneath it signed the name
"Nietzche." Another person came along and spray-painted an X over
the slogan and put in its place the words, "Nietzche is dead," and
signed it, "God."

In spite of the fact that the overwhelming majority of Americans
believe in God, He doesn't seem to make much difference in their
lives. For example, when making decisions, especially about moral
issues, very few people turn to God for guidance. Instead, we look to
ourselves for such guidance. Americans usually choose which commandments to believe and tend to think of God as "a general principle of life" or as a "distant and pale reflection of the God of our
forefathers."[1]

Nowhere is the crisis of faith more evident than in our homes.
Marriages are often troubled because there exists a God-shaped
vacuum in our lives that only He can fill. The sharing of a rich and

meaningful spiritual life together is the missing link of many modern marriages.

That may sound like an over-simplification of the problem, so let me explain. James Dobson noted the need for the spiritual enrichment of couples in an informal study he conducted of more than 600 people in which couples spoke candidly about the concepts and methods that have worked in their homes. According to Dobson, the couples "suggested that newlyweds should establish and maintain a *Christ-centered home.*" Everything rests on that foundation. If a young husband and wife are deeply committed to Jesus Christ, they enjoy enormous advantages over the family with no spiritual dimension.[2]

A Cord of Three Strands

Think of marriage like a braid of hair. At first glance, a braid of hair appears to be made of only two strands. Small children try to braid hair first by using only two strands. Of course, a braid cannot be woven out of two strands—three are required. The same is true of marriage. At first glance, marriage appears to be made of only two people—a husband and his wife—but three are actually present, a husband, a wife and God Himself. He is the third strand of the braid. This is what the biblical writer means when he says, *"A cord of three strands is not quickly broken."*[3]

No couple, in and of themselves, can love each other with the kind of covenant love we've been talking about. Only God can give us this kind of love for each other. The Apostle Paul reminds us of this truth: *"God has poured out his love into our hearts by the Holy Spirit, whom he has given us."*[4] God's love, poured supernaturally into our hearts, is the source of the unconditional love we share in the marriage covenant.

Couples today need to recapture the spiritual side of love if they hope to build marriages made to last. This is what Dietriech

Bonhoeffer had in mind when he wrote these inspiring words in a wedding service for his niece:

Marriage is more than your love for each other. It has a higher dignity and power, for it is God's holy ordinance, through which He wills to perpetuate the human race till the end of time. In your love you see only your two selves in the world, but in marriage you are a link in the chain of the generations, which God causes to come and to pass away to His glory, and calls into His kingdom. In your love you see only the heaven of your happiness, but in marriage you are placed at the post of responsibility towards the world and mankind. Your love is your own private possession, but marriage is more than something personal - it is a status, an office.[5]

THE COMPATIBILITY QUOTIENT

Most people would agree with the proposition that happily married couples are, by and large, compatible. The greater their compatibility, the better their chances of developing a lasting and fulfilling relationship. This fact accounts for the a variety of marital inventories designed to help engaged couples assess their level of compatibility before they get married.

Compatibility consists of a variety of factors including: family background, education, career goals, age, personality type, hobbies, core beliefs, values and ethics. Each of these can be measured on a scale ranging from highly incompatible to highly compatible.

While each area is important in the compatibility quotient, I think it's safe to say that the most important area is a couple's spirituality. By spirituality, I mean our most basic, fundamental beliefs, values and convictions that shape the way we live. What we are unwilling to compromise. How we make sense out of the world. What we consider sacred. The value we place on our relationships. All of this and more, makes up this thing called spirituality.

Now, when a couple is disconnected spiritually, their relationship exists on a surface level. While it is true that some couples are able to transcend their spiritual and religious differences to enjoy a satisfying relationship, most couples struggle in their marriage when they are spiritually incompatible.

DELIGHTFUL DIFFERENCES

The subject of spirituality is a hot topic, to say the least. First of all, not everyone defines spirituality the same way nor have we had the same spiritual experiences. So, the first rule of thumb is to value and respect each other's faith and values. Husbands and wives damage their relationship when they fail to show respect for each other's spiritual values and experiences.

I've come to learn that people experience God in different ways. Some experience Him through music and the arts. Others experience Him in worship services, Bible study and prayer. While others still experience God in nature, taking a walk or playing with their kids. The point is, we're all wired differently when it comes to our spiritual side.

The danger exists, then, of trying to force others to our own spiritual persuasion. Such actions come off as being judgmental and tears many marriages apart. I can't count the times I've listened to a husband or wife pour out their frustrations in a counseling session because they were being pressured about spiritual issues by their partner.

As a pastor, I've heard husbands make the apology, "I'm not on the same spiritual level as my wife," or "I don't know the Bible like she does." I always assure them, "God is not calling you to be where your wife is spiritually; He's calling you to a unique relationship with Him."

An interesting conversation took place between Jesus and Peter which occurred shortly after Jesus' resurrection. Three times Jesus asked him the question, "Do you love me?" Peter answered every time, "Lord, you know that I love you."

But something else of crucial importance was said during their conversation. At one point, Peter noticed John eavesdropping. So he asked Jesus, "What about him?" Jesus responded rather bluntly, "What is that to you? You must follow me."

Sometimes I think God says the same thing to husbands and wives who get caught up evaluating each other spiritually. "Lord, what about my wife?" "Lord, what about my husband?" God responds, "What is that to you? You follow me."

During a marriage seminar I conducted, a gentleman shared with the group how he and his wife came from different Christian backgrounds. He was more expressive in his worship while she was more reserved. They had been married about forty years. He told us how he had made a terrible mistake for about thirty-five years of their marriage trying to force his wife to be like him in the way she worshipped.

Then he added, "It wasn't until a few years ago that I came to value her vibrant walk with God and respect her for who she is." He went on to tell the group how God had miraculously worked in his life through his wife's prayers on his behalf. As a result, he came to experience a new-found respect for her.

This doesn't mean that a husband and wife aren't to have any spiritual influence on each other. Couples need to pray for each other, love each other and promote each other's spiritual growth. However, they must refrain from judging each other or trying to force one partner to conform to the other's measure of spiritual maturity. As Jesus said, "Judge not and you will not be judged."

I also need to point out that spiritual compatibility doesn't mean that a couple shares the same exact spiritual experiences or even agrees on every spiritual issue or moral conviction. While God certainly deals with us as couples, He also deals with us individually. Marriage doesn't negate each person's individual relationship to God. We need to be careful to remember that no two people grow spiritually in an identical fashion. So, we need to give each other the freedom to grow in our faith at our pace. When we do, we move from pressure to peace in marriage.

One of the most important lessons I've learned is to trust what God is doing in you partner's life. God finishes what He starts in all our lives. One of the most reassuring verses in the Bible says, *"Being confident of this, that He who began a good work in you will carry it on to completion until the day of Christ Jesus."*[6] This means that the prayer we need to pray is not, "Lord, change my partner," but rather, "Lord, change *me*."

It's The Relationship, Stupid!

Defining spirituality is a fairly difficult task in itself. But let's try to get a handle on it. David Benner says that spirituality is "the response to a deep and mysterious human yearning for self-transcendence and surrender."[7] You may say, "Put that in my language." Simply put, spirituality is our inner longing for a relationship with God. As Gothe said, "All human longing is really the longing for God."

Some people, however, have never identified the nature of this longing. They try to satisfy it with power, prestige, possessions or pleasure. But the answer is summed up best in Augustine's famous prayer: "Our soul is restless until it finds rest in You, O Lord. For You have made us for Yourself."[8]

It's easy to make the mistake of defining spirituality in terms of what we do—Bible study, church attendance, prayer, family devotions, helping the poor, serving others and so forth. However, spirituality is measured more in terms of who we are than what we do. Don't misunderstand me. All these activities are important and virtuous. But spirituality runs deeper. Sometimes we confuse the *means* with the *end*. While the *means* of spirituality certainly involves such activities, the *end* is to experience God in a living and dynamic relationship.

Here's my point: Couples may indeed participate in any number of spiritual activities yet lack a meaningful spiritual relationship together. The issue I'm raising is one of *quality* rather than *quantity*. In other words, how often we attend church is not as important as what happens to us when we attend. How often we pray is not as important as how prayer enriches our lives. How much of the Bible we read each day is not as important as whether or not we receive any positive benefits from reading it.

After all, what difference does it make if a couple attends church together but treat each other harshly as they drive out of the parking lot? What benefit is Bible reading and prayer around the dinner table if we don't treat each other as Christ treats us? What virtue is there in confessing our needs to God if we can't talk openly to each other about how we feel? You see, true spirituality concerns our relationships with others as well as God. This is exactly why Jesus inseparably bound together the two commandments: Love the Lord your God and love your neighbor as yourself.

I met my wife Barbie for the first time on a blind date. From the moment I laid eyes on her I was head over heels in love with her. You may think I'm exaggerating for literary purposes, but I'm not. And, believe me, I wanted to get to know her. I didn't merely want to know about her; I wanted to know her—to share my life with her and for her to share her life with me.

So, it is with God. He wants us to really know Him personally and intimately. There are some fascinating snapshots of people in the Bible who knew God this way. Enoch walked with God. Abraham was known as the friend of God. God spoke with Moses face to face as a man speaks to his friend. King David was known as a man after God's own heart. Jesus said to his disciples, "I no longer call you servants...I call you friends." And Paul the Apostle summed his entire spiritual desire by saying simply, "I want to know Christ."[9]

During the 1992 presidential election, Bill Clinton and his campaign committee said to George Bush, his opponent, "It's the economy, stupid!" Well, when it comes to spiritual living, we need to remember, "It's the relationship!"

SCIENCE IS CATCHING UP

Researchers studying successful marriages are discovering more and more the importance of couples sharing common beliefs and values. Similar values, ethnic backgrounds, interests, IQs, religions and lifestyles may be the most important ingredients in lasting relationships according to Frank Pittman, Atlanta-based psychiatrist and author of *Private Lies: Infidelity and the Betrayal of Intimacy.*[10]

David H. Olson, professor of family and social science at the University of Minnesota, says that shared attitudes are so vital that it's possible to predict as early as the day a couple gets engaged whether their marriage will last. He based his findings on a study involving 164 dating couples who responded to questions about their values. He interviewed them again three years later and found that 52 of them had never married, and of those who did, 31 had already separated, while 22 described their relationship as unhappy. After reviewing all the initial interviews, Olson was able to identify which couples were seriously mismatched on the basis of their shared attitudes and values.[11]

The importance of couples sharing their faith together can't be overstated. Some advocate that religion is strictly a personal matter.

Not so. Religion is relational in nature. Religion concerns our relationship with God and our relationships with others, especially those in our family. Faith begins at home.

Research shows that Americans are still, by and large, people of faith. George Gallup, Jr. and Jim Castelli in *The People's Religion: American Faith in the Nineties,* report that 98 percent of Americans believe in the existence of God, 73 percent believe in life after death, 86 percent have full or substantial faith in the Bible as divinely inspired, and 74 percent favor a constitutional amendment to allow voluntary school prayer.[12] Furthermore, in a 1991 City University of New York study, nearly 90 percent of Americans identified themselves as either Christians or Jews; only 7.5 percent claimed no religion at all.

In spite of these encouraging signs, we are witnessing an everwidening gap between what might be called *inherited faith* and *integrated faith*. For example, while pollsters report that 98 percent of Americans believe in God only 67 percent say there is no such thing as absolute truth.[13] Figure that out if you can. *Inherited faith* is faith that is handed down from one generation to another without thoughtful assimilation by succeeding generations. Such faith exists as a creed, a family tradition or religious ritualism but lacks the life-changing power of a personal relationship with God. On the other hand, *integrated faith* is faith that a person has received from others but has been embraced personally. It stands tried and proved by way of personal experience. When a husband and wife share together their deeply-rooted personal faith in God, their relationship achieves the highest form of intimacy known in marriage.

The Hebrew *shema* (meaning *hear*) expresses the need for sharing our faith at home: *"These commandments that I give you today are to be upon your hearts. Impress them on your children. Talk about them when you sit at home and when you walk along the road, when you lie down and when you get up.*"[14] One survey poll indicates that 60 percent of all Americans hold to their religious beliefs because of the example of their parents.

Tragically, however, families are neglecting religious training at home. According to a Gallup poll, this is what American adults said when asked if they received religious training while growing up at home: In 1968, only 9 percent said they received no religious training; in 1978, 17 percent cited no religious training, and in 1988, 25 percent said they received no religious training. Also, in 1988, 49 percent of parents polled said their children were receiving no spiritual or religious training.[15]

As secularism continues to spread its tentacles through every facet of American culture, sharing our faith at home becomes more crucial than ever before.

THE PATHWAY TO INTIMACY

Couples frequently complain about the lack of intimacy in their relationship. Not sexual intimacy but emotional intimacy. They communicate on a surface level. They don't share their innermost thoughts, dreams and fears. Consequently, they live like emotional strangers in the same house.

When we learn that God loves us as we are and that He accepts us unconditionally, then we are willing to open up to Him in prayer and confession. As we come to know God's love, we are free to express ourselves without fear of rejection, judgment or manipulation. This is what Genesis means when it describes the intimacy of Adam and Eve: *"The man and his wife were both naked, and they felt no shame."*[16] Their closeness to God brought a rich intimacy in which they felt safe to share everything. But when they sinned, the scenario changed. The Bible says they became afraid and hid themselves. We've been hiding from God and from others ever since; afraid to openly express ourselves.

John Powell wrote a thought-provoking book on this very issue entitled, *Why Am I Afraid To Tell You Who I Am?* The book made a profound impact on me when I was freshman in college. We've all struggled with the question, Why am I afraid to tell you who I am? The answer is, If I let you see the real Me, you may not like it, and that's all I have to offer.

As Ralph Waldo Emerson said, "There is no terror like that of being known." So instead of being ourselves, we project an image in an effort to be who we think others want us to be. We do this so that others will love and accept us. Unfortunately, we get caught in the trap of constantly changing our image to meet our perception of other people's expectations. The real person gets lost somewhere in the process.

On a humorous note, I heard that when we're in our twenties, we worry about what people think of us. In our forties, we don't care what they think of us. In our sixties, we discover that they haven't been thinking of us at all!

When we suffer hurt and rejection, we tend to retreat inside a shell, refusing to run the risk of getting hurt again. The cure for the fear of rejection starts with experiencing the unconditional love of God. The Bible says, *"Perfect love casts out fear."* As we become more aware of God's love and our partner's love, we become more trusting. And trust is the basis of intimacy in any relationship, especially marriage.

HANDLING THE HEAT

Not only does spirituality enhance a couple's intimacy, it also enables them to handle life when it hurts. In Lewis Carroll's classic, *Alice In Wonderland*, the white knight tried to anticipate all the problems that might await him as he prepared for his journey. To withstand the attacks of lions, he covered his horse with sheets of steel.

To protect his horse from alligators, the knight attached knives to the legs of his horse. By the time the horse and rider were protected against all possible dangers, the horse collapsed under the weight!

So it is with us. We try everything in our power to shield ourselves from life's adversities only to collapse under the weight. The issue is not whether we will face tough times, but rather how we handle them when they come. Couples who share a rich and meaningful faith handle the adversities of life better than those without faith — plain and simple.

When the noted agnostic Robert Ingersol died, the funeral notice read: "There will be no singing at the funeral." There was nothing to sing about. No resource of faith in the crucible of life. No song of praise in the valley of the shadow.

How different was my experience at the funeral of one of my parishioners who died of cancer in her mid-forties. She had battled cancer for some time. In spite of her illness, she possessed a vibrant faith which she shared openly and freely with everyone she met.

The day of her funeral her husband told me how inspired he had been by her faith. He said, "I would often stand next to her in church—knowing she was in tremendous pain—yet as we sang, she would sing praises and give glory to God." Then he added, "She had peace in the midst of her pain."

How many couples end up in divorce because they can't handle the crushing pressures of life? We need spiritual resources to help us through these times. Or, to use the words of Scripture we need, "grace to help in the time of need."

You see, the greatest resource God gives us is the power of faith. You attitude determines your altitude. Your faith determines your fortitude. Psychologist Albert Ellis' A-B-C theory helps illustrate how our beliefs affect the way we handle the heat.[17] I've outlined it below:

$$A \quad + \quad B \quad = \quad C$$

A	+	B	=	C
ACTIVATING		BELIEF		EMOTIONAL
EXPERIENCE		SYSTEM		CONSEQUENCE

In his model, *A* stands for the *activating experience* (what happens to us), *B* stands for our *belief system* (how we interpret the problem) and *C* stands for our *emotional consequence* (how we feel). According to Ellis, it is a faulty assumption to believe that *A* (what happens to us) causes *C* (how we feel). The intervening variable is *B*—our perception, interpretation or belief about what happens to us. The circumstances of life do not determine our level of emotional suffering or our happiness; rather what we believe about what happens to us ultimately determines how we feel. Feeling is subject to thinking.

Here's a formula to remember when tough times come your way:

> ***PROBLEM + PERCEPTION = PAIN OR PEACE***

We make the choice between victory or defeat by the way we react to the situations of life. That's good news because it means we are in control of our emotional state rather than being victims of what happens to us.

Corrie Ten Boom, survivor of Hitler's death camps, learned how to tap into the triumphant power of faith. In her autobiography *Tramp For The Lord*, she shares this anonymous poem that helps us put life's adversities into perspective:

My life is but a weaving, between my God and me.
I do not choose the colors, He worketh steadily.
Offtimes He weaveth sorrow, and I in foolish pride,
Forget He sees the upper, and I the underside.
Not till the loom is silent, and shuttles cease to fly,
Will God unroll the canvas and explain the reason why.
The dark threads are as needful in the skillful Weaver's hand,
As the threads of gold and silver in the pattern He has planned.

A few years ago I sat spellbound as I listened via radio to a Chinese pastor who had been imprisoned for his faith. While in prison, he witnessed for Christ to the other prisoners and to the prison guards. Many of them accepted Christ as their Savior. So, his captors sought to silence him by placing him in solitary confinement. He was forbidden a Bible, not allowed to pray or to sing and was shut off from the other prisoners to prevent him from preaching.

In addition, he was assigned the job of working the cesspool. Alone. The first day he stepped into the cesspool and the door slammed shut behind him, he realized quickly how blessed he was. Since no one could hear him, he could pray and sing as loud and as long as he wanted. Month after month he enjoyed rich fellowship with God in the cesspool.

He said his favorite song to sing in the cesspool was the hymn, "In The Garden."[18] As he reflected on his years in prison, he began to cite the first verse over the radio airwaves:

I come to the garden alone, while the dew is still on the roses,
And the voice I hear falling on my ear, the Son of God discloses.
And He walks with me and He talks with me,
And He tells me I am His own.
And the joy we share as we tarry there, none other has ever known.

Then he said to the interviewer, "I survived those years alone in prison because I learned to turn a cesspool into a garden."

Whatever stress, or loss or difficulty you face in life, you too can turn the cesspool into a garden and know beyond a shadow of a doubt: *In all things God works for your good.*

No Atheists In Foxholes

You're probably asking right now, What can a couple do to develop their faith together? Well, it all starts with prayer. When you stop and think about it, prayer can be one of the most intimate experiences a couple has together. When we pray—I mean, really pray— we become transparent before God as we tell Him our deepest struggles, questions and needs with gut-level honesty. To do that in the presence of another person is risky business—it takes a lot of faith not only in God but also in the person we're praying with.

Nearly everyone prays, in one way or another. Especially, when times are tough. As the saying goes, "There are no atheists in fox-holes." According to a *Newsweek* survey, 54 percent of American adults say they pray every day. Twenty-nine percent pray more than once a day. Eighty-seven percent believe God answers their prayers at least some of the time.[19]

What really is prayer? Prayer is simply the process of talking and listening to God. Rosalind Rinker says, "Prayer is the expression of the human heart in conversation with God. The more natural the prayer, the more real He becomes. It has all been simplified for me to this extent: Prayer is a dialogue between two persons who love each other." I like her definition.

We ask ourselves, Does prayer really work? More importantly, can prayer actually enhance a couple's marriage? Will it make them happier, or improve their communication skills, or deepen their intimacy, or build their trust, or strengthen their love, or help them deal with the pressures of daily living? The answer is unequivocally, Yes!

The problem with many people is they only use prayer as a last resort. It's like the story of a ship that got caught in a great storm at sea. As the storm raged, the captain realized his ship was sinking fast. He called out, "Does anyone know how to pray?"

One man stepped forward. "Aye, Captain, I know how to pray."

"Good," said the Captain, "you pray while the rest of us put on our life jackets—we're one short."

But prayer is more than a last resort; it is our lifeline to God. We can live as well spiritually without praying as we can physically without breathing. A husband and wife need to pray often for each other and with each other. Now, I am well aware of the fact that praying together can be an awkward experience. Also, time-demands, schedule conflicts and telephone disruptions wreak havoc in trying to maintain regular family devotions.

I'm reminded of an incident that occurred in our home when my daughter Charlsi was about five years old. She and I were downstairs in the family room while Barbie and David Paul were upstairs. I said to her, "Charlsi, tell your mother and David Paul it's time for our family devotion." She proceeded to walk to the bottom of the stairs and called out, "Hey, guys, come downstairs. Dad says it's time for our family *commotion*."

Well, sometimes it may turn out more like a commotion than a devotion but push through the disruptions and the awkward feelings as you discover the power of praying together.

I'm sure you've heard the slogan, "Prayer changes things." The greater truth is—"Prayer changes me." Time and time again, when I have presented a situation to God in prayer, He has changed the prayer agenda from the situation I'm praying about to dealing with me personally. As George Meredith observed, "He who rises from prayer a better man, his prayer is answered."

Here are some prayer tips you may find helpful as you develop your prayer life:

- Prayer is more than talking to God; it's listening to God.
- Prayer is moving from trying to control God to allowing Him to direct you.
- Prayer is more than something you do; it's Someone you are with.
- Prayer is not a journey to God; it's a journey with God.
- Prayer is unbroken communion with God whereby you am continually aware of His presence, sensitive to His voice and obedient to His direction.

Most of all, remember that prayer is not a way that we manipulate God into doing what we want. Sometimes what we way is not the best thing for us. To the contrary, prayer brings us into alignment with the will of God for our lives. As Jesus taught us to pray, "Thy will be done."

During the Civil War, an unknown soldier penned this prayer to help us understand this principle.

I asked God for strength that I might achieve.
I was made weak that I might learn humbly to obey.

I asked God for health that I might do greater things.
I was given infirmity that I might do better things.

I asked for riches that I might be happy.
I was given poverty that I might be wise.

I asked for power that I might have the praise of men.
I was given life that I might enjoy all things.

I got nothing that I asked for—but everything I had hoped for.
Almost despite myself, my unspoken prayers were answered.

I am among all men most richly blessed.

One final note: Prayer is only complete when we do our part to make our prayers come to pass. Its like the slogan soldiers were fond of saying during the Revolutionary War: "Trust in God but keep your gunpowder dry." Faith is no substitute for action. And neither is prayer. Never pray a prayer unless you are willing to be part of the answer.

The greatest prayer ever prayed was given to us by Jesus. We call it the Lord's Prayer. I want to encourage you to pray it daily because, in reality, it teaches us how to live in a right relationship with God and others. It covers every aspect of our lives. The way we pray determines the way we live. Reflect on the richness of the Lord's Prayer and its call to action:

The Lord's Prayer and You

I cannot say **Our,**
   if my religion has no room for others, and their needs.
I cannot say **Father,**
   if I do not demonstrate this relationship in my daily living.
I cannot say **Who art in heaven,**
   if all my interests and pursuits are in earthly things.
I cannot say **Hallowed be Thy name,**
   if I, who am called by His name am not holy.
I cannot say **Thy kingdom come,**
   if I am unwilling to give up my own sovereignty and accept
   the righteous reign of God.
I cannot say **Thy will be done,**
   if I am unwilling or resentful of having it in my own life.
I cannot say **On earth as it is in heaven,**
   unless I am truly ready to give myself to His service here
   and now.
I cannot say **Give us this day our daily bread,**
   without expending honest effort for it, or by ignoring the
   genuine needs of my fellowmen.
I cannot say **Forgive us our trespasses,**
   as we forgive those who trespass against us, if I continue
   to harbor a grudge against anyone.
I cannot say **Lead us not into temptation,**
   if I deliberately choose to remain in a situation where I am
   likely to be tempted.
I cannot say **Deliver us from evil,**
   if I am not prepared to fight in the spiritual realm with the
   weapon of prayer.
I cannot say **Thine is the kingdom,**
   if I do not give the King the disciplined obedience of a loyal
   subject.

*I cannot say **Thine is the power**,*

   if I fear what my neighbors and friends may say or do.

*I cannot say **Thine is the glory**,*

   if I am seeking my own glory first.

*I cannot say **Forever**,*

   if I am too anxious about each day's affairs.

*I cannot say **Amen**,*

   unless I honestly say, "Come what may, this is my prayer."

Author Unknown

CHAPTER EIGHT

TWENTY-FOUR HOUR FORGIVENESS

IN THOMAS HARDY'S CLASSIC, *TESS OF THE D'URBERVILLES*, TESS IS A young bride who gambles her future happiness on her husband's ability to forgive her. On their wedding night she confesses to him her affair in a past relationship with another man. As he hears her words, his countenance changes, his heart hardens and his gaze becomes a cold stare of disbelief. He lacks the power to forgive. What could have been a beautiful relationship dies from a lack of love.

Jesus taught us to pray, "Forgive us our debts as we forgive our debtors." It's not enough to be *forgiven;* we need to be *forgiving.* But that can be a challenge. As the rhyme goes:

To live above with saints we love,
　　Oh that will be glory.
To live below with saints we know,
　　now that's a different story!

Marriage is the art of 24-hour forgiveness. Mark Twain said, "Forgiveness is the fragrance the rose leaves on the heel that crushed it." There is simply no way to talk about marriage as a covenant without including forgiveness. Forgiveness sustains the covenant through the severest of storms of married life.

A Luxury You Can't Afford

Let's be completely honest—no couple can afford the luxury of unforgiveness. The price is just too high. Unforgiveness eats away at a relationship like a cancer. To put it frankly, unforgiveness is a terminal disease to any marriage. Perhaps the Bible gives us the best insights into the destructive power unforgiveness plays in our lives and relationships.[1] It tells us that...

1. **Unforgiveness blocks the flow of God's forgiveness in our lives:** *"For if you forgive men when they sin against you, your heavenly Father will also forgive you. But if you do not forgive men their sins, your Father will not forgive your sins."*

2. **Unforgiveness hinders our prayers:** *"And when you stand praying, if you hold anything against anyone, forgive him, so that your Father in heaven may forgive you your sins."*

3. **Unforgiveness is like a spiritual boomerang:** *"Do not judge, or you too will be judged. For in the same way you judge others, you will be judged, and with the measure you use, it will be measured to you."*

4. **Unforgiveness poisons our relationships:** *"See to it that no one misses the grace of God and that no bitter root grows up to cause trouble and defile many."*

Some people simply refuse to give up a grudge. It's like the story of two sisters, Matilda and Alice, who held a grudge against each other for years. They cut off all communications. Then Matilda got deathly ill and was hospitalized. So, Alice felt obligated to go visit her.

As Alice entered the hospital room, Matilda looked sternly at her with a cold stare. At last she said in a faint voice, "The doctors say

I'm seriously ill, Alice. If I pass away, I want you to know you're forgiven. But if I pull through, things stay the way they are!"

Some people are fond of the old Irish prayer:

May those who love us, love us;
And those who don't love us,
May God turn their hearts;
And if He doesn't turn their hearts,
May He turn their ankles,
So we'll know them by their limping.

Obviously, none of us are interested in living in unforgiveness so let's get to the task at hand—learning the art of 24-hour forgiveness.

WHATEVER BECAME OF SIN?

All this talk about marriage as a covenant and unconditional love seems so idealistic. Is it realistic to think that a couple can live together without making demands and expectations of each other? Are we even capable of loving unconditionally, overlooking each other's faults and turning the other cheek when we've been wronged?

Whether we want to admit it or not, in spite of our best intentions, we often fall back into a contractual relationship. We bargain and negotiate to get what we want. We make deals and strive for compromises. We keep a secret "wish list" of expectations hoping one day to get our partner to meet all our needs.

The problem we confront in marriage is a three-letter word—*sin*. Psychiatrist Karl Menninger posed the question, Whatever became of sin? Sin went to the psychiatrist and became a disorder. Sin visited the physician and became a disease. Sin encountered the sociologist and became an environmental response. Sin went to the educator and became a learning disorder.

Today, it's almost politically incorrect to even talk about sin. Doug

Marlette observes the moral absurdity of our times in his parody of "Amazing Grace:"

Amazing grace how sweet the sound,
   that saved a stunted self-concept like me.
I once was stressed-out, but now am empowered,
   I was visually challenged, but now I see.

Our reluctance to admit our sins against God and others has resulted in a "no-fault" society. The cry of the age is, "It's not my fault!" We have no-fault car insurance, no-fault divorces and, now, no-fault moral choices.

We love to play the Blame Game. The game started back in Eden. When Adam and Eve sinned God confronted them, "What have you done?" Adam blurts out, "The *woman* you put here with me, gave me some of the fruit." He blamed Eve and God in one fell swoop. The God confronted Eve. She made the excuse, "The serpent deceived me." And, of course, the serpent didn't have a leg to stand on!

Anna Russell, the British comedian, confronts our problem head-on in her poem "Jolly Old Sigmund Freud:"

I went to my psychiatrist to be psychoanalyzed,
To find out why I kicked the cat, and blackened my wife's eyes.
He laid me on his downy couch to see what he could find,
And this is what he dredged up from my subconscious mind.
When I was one my mama hid my dolly in a trunk,
And so it falls naturally that I am always drunk.
When I was two I suffered from ambivalence toward my brothers,
And so it falls naturally I poisoned all my lovers.
Now I am so glad that I have learned the lessons this has taught,
That everything I do that's wrong, is someone else's fault.[2]

Then the Bible speaks and tells us that the first step to recovery is to admit we're wrong. The psalmist David said, *"Surely I was sinful at birth."* And the Apostle Paul adds, *"All have sinned."* The only people who don't believe in original sin are those who have never raised a two-year old!

So, what is sin? The word sin basically means *to miss the mark.* The Bible tells us that sin is unbelief, neglect of opportunity, transgression of God's law and all unrighteous acts.[3] We even talk about sins of commission, deliberate acts, and sins of omission, neglecting one's duties and responsibilities. When the Sunday School teacher asked the kindergartners, "What are sins of omission?" Little Johnny responded confidently, "Those are sins we could've committed but didn't."

We all struggle with sin. We make mistakes. Violate God's law. Contradict our own consciences. Shade the truth. Tell little white lies. Harbor hidden resentments. Wish harm to another. Envy other people's success. And on and on.

Pierre, one of the central characters in Tolstoy's classic *War and Peace,* cries out to God: "Why is it that I know what is right and I do what is wrong?" We've all asked that question.

My daughter Charlsi, who was five years old at the time, and I were driving home one day after running a few errands. Out of the blue she said to me, "Dad, what I can't figure out is whether we're the good guys or the bad guys!" (To this day I have no idea what prompted her question.)

I told her, "Sweetheart, Jesus lives in our hearts and He helps us to be good."

She thought about that for a second and said, "Sometimes we're both good guys and bad guys, aren't we?"

Well said. She put her finger on our problem. Sometimes we're both good guys and bad guys.

So, how do we deal with sin when it affects our marriages? Or, to use Charlsi's words, How do we keep it together when we act like bad guys instead of good guys?

Forgiveness is the key. Just as God forgives us our sins, we must forgive each other if we expect to experience the power of a covenant together. When we think about forgiveness we can't help but ask some important questions like...

- What is forgiveness?
- How do you know when you've forgiven someone?
- Does forgiveness automatically take away our feelings of hurt and anger?
- Does God really expect us to forgive everybody?
- Are there any limits to forgiveness, like in cases of adultery, abuse or abandonment?

Since the Bible is basically a book about forgiveness let's look inside it's pages for our answers. We need to start with a workable definition. So, here goes: *Forgiveness means to cancel the debt, to restore the relationship and to bless the person who hurt us*. Let's take a closer look at these three faces of forgiveness.

CANCEL THE DEBT

One day Jesus' told a fascinating story about forgiveness. Peter asked him, "Lord, how many times shall I forgive my brother when he sins against me? Up to seven times?" He thought he was being generous with his forgiveness. That is until he heard Jesus' response: "I tell you, not seven times, but seven times seven." In other words, forgive those who hurt you an infinite number of times. God's forgiveness has no limits so neither should yours.

Listen carefully to His explanation of forgiveness:

Therefore, the kingdom of heaven is like a king who wanted to settle accounts with his servants. As he began the settlement, a man who owed him ten thousand talents was brought to him. Since he was not able to pay, the master ordered that he and his wife and his children and all that he had be sold to repay the debt.

The servant fell on his knees before him. "Be patient with me," he begged, "and I will pay back everything." The servant's master took pity on him, canceled the debt and let him go.

But when that servant went out, he found one of his fellow servants who owed him a hundred denarii. He grabbed him and began to choke him. "Pay back what you owe me!" he demanded.

His fellow servant fell to his knees and begged him, "Be patient with me, and I will pay you back."

But he refused. Instead, he went off and had the man thrown into prison until he could pay the debt. When the other servants saw what had happened, they were greatly distressed and went and told their master everything that had happened.

Then the master called the servant in. "You wicked servant," he said, "I canceled all that debt of yours because you begged me to. Shouldn't you have had mercy on your fellow servant just as I had on you?" In anger his master turned him over to the jailers to be tortured, until he should pay back all he owed.

This is how my heavenly Father will treat each of you unless you forgive your brother from your heart.[4]

Thought-provoking, isn't it? He tells of a certain man who was unable to pay off his debt. So he pleaded for mercy. So the mortgage holder had mercy on the man and canceled his debt. Forgiveness, then, is best understood from a financial sense. Most of us understand the tremendous load that is lifted off our shoulders when a debt is paid off. That's exactly what it means to forgive somebody —

to cancel the debt and lift off the load of guilt, shame and failure. (Maybe you're thinking right now that you wish your credit card company understood forgiveness!)

Now, when we apply this truth to our relationships we get a clear mental picture of forgiveness in action. Canceling a person's debt means to forget the matter, to release the right to resentment, to forfeit the privilege of revenge, to give up any grudge, to remove all guilt and to pardon all sin.

I once listened to a person tell me in a counseling session, "I have the right to take revenge." "Not if you're a Christian," I responded. In Christ we forfeit that right. Shall we, whose great debt of sin against God has been canceled, refuse to cancel the debts of those who have sinned against us? Are we justified in receiving something from God which we are unwilling to give to others? Remember Jesus' words, *"Freely you have received; freely give."*

Here's a letter I received from a wife who learned to cancel the debt she held against her husband:

Dear Dr. Cooper,

I want to thank you for all your concern for my marriage and for taking the time to counsel with my husband. The Lord has shown me a very important characteristic of Himself, through my circumstance.

Tuesday night the Lord revealed to me something I had never considered…Through all the apparent lack of love from my husband I had totally overlooked God's key to freedom. Let me explain.

Recently, I started reading a book on forgiveness. The author writes of the power God releases when we lay down our rights. Through forgiveness we lay down our rights. To forgive is: (1) to give up the wish (desire) to punish or get even, (2) to give up all claim to, and (3) to not demand payment for.

I saw for the first time a different aspect of what Jesus did on the cross. When God created me He knew exactly what choices I would make and what sins I would commit; yet He created me anyway. Why? Because He already had forgiven me! He chose to forgive me (and the world).

God has shown me that forgiveness is the most important factor in restoring relationships—that is what He did for us.

The key to forgiveness is to forgive before forgiveness is asked for by the offender. Jesus died for me before I was even able to ask for forgiveness from Him.

I have such an excitement for what God is going to do in my life, marriage, and family. I wish everyone could see what forgiveness can do in their lives if they are willing to not demand that God serve judgment on their offenders.

RESTORE THE RELATIONSHIP

Forgiveness also means to restore the wounded relationship. God's forgiveness restores our fractured relationship with Him caused by sin. The word *reconciliation* describes this restoration process. To be reconciled means to move from a state of animosity and hostility to one of friendship and peace. Paul explains Christ's crucifixion by saying, *"God was reconciling the world to Himself in Christ, not counting men's sins against them."* What is more, God *"gave us the ministry of reconciliation."*[5] What better place for the ministry of reconciliation to take place than in marriage?

Jesus stressed the importance of reconciling broken relationships. In the Sermon on the Mount He says, *"If you are offering your gift at the altar and there remember that your brother has something against you, leave your gift there in front of the altar. First go and be reconciled to your brother; then come and offer your gift."*[6] The words,

"First go and be reconciled," leap off the page. Jesus is saying, in no uncertain terms, that we cannot be in right relationship with God unless our relationships with others are in order.

This is why He inseparably tied the command, "Love your neighbor as yourself," to the greatest commandment, "Love the Lord your God with all your heart." You can't have one without the other. Since we have been reconciled to God, we must be reconciled to others.

It needs to be pointed out that extenuating circumstances can prevent the restoration of certain relationships. The Bible says, *"If it is possible, as far as it depends on you, live at peace with everyone."*[7] That's reasonable advice with which we can all live. The reason he adds the disclaimer, "If it is possible," is because he knows full well that living at peace with some people remains an impossibility in this life. God requires only that we do everything within our power to be reconciled when relationships are fractured. The person on the other end of our attempts at reconciliation may or may not respond.

People who have been abused in a marriage often ask if forgiveness means that they are obligated to stay in such a destructive relationship. Or, if they are separated on account of abuse if they should go back. The answer on both counts is *No*.

God does not require any person to submit to abuse in any form. Such a notion of submission that requires either a husband or a wife to remain in an abusive situation is, in itself, abusive. Just because you forgive someone does not mean you have to return to that destructive relationship. My point is that restoration has limitations. While we are able to forgive we're not always able to put a relationship back together.

Another crucial question that comes up is how can we forgive a parent or significant other who is now deceased. We can forgive them in prayer. That simply means to bring the person to God in prayer and declare that you forgive them. Praying the prayer of forgiveness will free your heart from resentment, unforgiveness and repressed anger.

Here's another important issue we face: How can a divorced couple who have no plans of getting remarried restore their relationship? Obviously, if either of them is remarried reconciliation won't involve a restoration of their marriage. Even the Old Testament forbids such reconfigurations of marriage after divorce and remarriage has occurred.[8] However, reconciliation should be sought along the lines of forgiving each other and releasing all feelings and thoughts of ill-will, anger and resentment. Any personal interactions with a former spouse should reflect the meekness and gentleness of Christ characterized by courtesy, compassion and concern. Treating each other as Christ treats us is the heart of the matter in restoring the relationship, not necessarily getting back together.

Perhaps Jesus' story of the Prodigal Son illustrates best what it means to restore a broken relationship. After the prodigal son comes to his senses and realizes what a colossal mess he's made out of his life, he says to himself, "I will set out and go back to my father and say to him: 'Father, I have sinned against heaven and against you. I am no longer worthy to be called your son; make me like one of your hired men.'"

Why does he make such a statement? Because he cannot fathom a forgiveness great enough to restore his relationship with his father like it was before he left.

As far as he was concerned, his youthful rebellion and indulgent lifestyle, which had cost him his inheritance and left him penniless, was enough to permanently ruin their relationship.

Now for the rest of the story:

So he got up and went to his father. But while he was still a long way off, his father saw him and was filled with compassion for him; he ran to his son, threw his arms around him and kissed him. The son said to him, "Father I have sinned against heaven and against you. I am no longer worthy to be called your son." But the father said to his servants, "Quick! Bring the best robe and put it on him. Put a ring on his finger and sandals on his feet. Bring the fattened calf and kill it. Let's have a feast and celebrate. For this son of mine was dead and is alive again; he was lost and is found."[9]

Notice something profound in this story. The prodigal refers to himself as a servant. But his father calls him, "my son." There's a world of difference between a servant and a son. The power of the father's forgiveness fully restored their relationship as if it had never been severed. And that is what it means for us to forgive.

BLESS THE OFFENDER

Not only do we cancel the debt and try to restore the relationship as best as possible, we must also bless the person who hurt us. What? You gotta be kidding! you may be saying right now. Hear me out on this point. I know it certainly goes against the grain of human nature. Yet, the ability to bless those who hurt us truly mirrors God's forgiveness toward us. As Martin Luther said, "My heart is too glad and too great to be the enemy of any man."

Forgiveness is only complete when the victim blesses the offender. That sounds backwards doesn't it? I mean, shouldn't the offender to do something kind for the victim? Well, that helps too but it doesn't take away the victim's responsibility to express kindness. Here are some suggestions: Send a card or a gift. Schedule lunch meeting or make a phone call to say, "I forgive you." Forgiveness is not a feeling; its an action. Do something tangible to express forgiveness, if at all possible.

The Bible says, *"Do not be overcome by evil, but overcome evil with good."*[10] What act of goodness can you do to overcome the evil committed against you? Jesus presents us with a sobering yet liberating commandment, *"Love your enemies, do good to those who hate you, bless those who curse you, pray for those who mistreat you."*[11] Notice the action words: **Love. Do good. Bless. Pray.**

I've got to share a story with you that I think you'll find incredible. During my first pastorate, one of my members was served divorce papers by her husband. He was having an affair with his secretary. So, he decided to leave his wife and their two children to marry the "other woman." Of course, she was devastated. She tried everything in her power to save their marriage but in time, the divorce was final.

After months of battling grief and depression, she began putting her life back together. One day she called me at my office and said, "Pastor, I just wanted you to know what I'm doing tonight and ask you to pray for me."

"What, exactly, are you planning to do tonight?" I asked.

She said, "I'm preparing dinner for my ex-husband and his new wife to show forgiveness to them. I know it will be difficult but I need to meet with them face to face and tell them that I forgive them."

Please understand, I'm not recommending her strategy to anyone. Such a course of action could be very risky to say the least. But I do want to underscore the fact that she demonstrated the courage to do what she needed to do in order to free herself from the trap of unforgiveness by blessing those who had deeply hurt her.

PUTTING IT ALL TOGETHER

Now we have a forgiveness formula: *Forgiveness is an act of the will by which we cancel the debt, restore the relationship and bless the offender.* Write it down or commit it to memory. It will come in handy.

I want to close this chapter by giving you eleven steps for conquering resentment by one of my favorite authors, E. Stanley Jones:[12]

1. *Remember that resentments have no part nor lot with a Christian. You cannot hold both Christ and resentments. Whether justified or unjustified, resentments are disastrous to the inner life—they are poison.*

2. *Remember that no one has ever treated you worse than you have treated God, and yet He forgives and forgets.*

3. *Remember the three levels of life and decide which one you are going to live on: (1) the demonic—return evil for good; (2) the human—return evil for evil; or (3) the divine—return good for evil.*

4. *Don't let the actions and attitudes of others determine your conduct and attitudes.*

5. *Remember to "shake off the dust." We are not to let the attitudes of people cling to us. There must be full and free forgiveness with no strings attached.*

6. *This does not mean that you have to like people and what they do to you. We are to see in others what they are to become.*

7. *Go beyond praying for people who do you wrong—bless them in His name.*

8. *Remember that the sum total of reality is behind you when you love—you are behind when you hate.*

9. *Don't fight your resentments—surrender them.*

10. *In surrendering your resentments to God you may have to expose them to man.*

11. *Then, be so inwardly outgoing and happy that resentments can have no part or lot in you.*

He follows these steps with four affirmations. Read them aloud and you let the power of forgiveness fill your heart.

- *Today I shall treat everybody as Christ treats me.*
- *I shall overcome evil with good, darkness with light, hate with love.*
- *I will not descend to the level of the person who has wronged me by trying to pay him back.*
- *I am so rich in forgiveness that I can afford to give it freely to others.*

When we forgive, we turn moral tragedies into marital triumphs. This anonymous piece entitled *Resemblance* says it best:

We are most like beasts when we kill.

We are most like men when we judge.

We are most like God when we forgive.

Remember, marriage is the art of 24-hour forgiveness.

CHAPTER NINE

JUMP-STARTING YOUR MARRIAGE

A FEW YEARS AGO OUR FAMILY TOOK A VACATION TO ARIZONA. WE wanted to relive the days of the old West. On our way to Old Tucson we drove through the beautiful saguaro cactus forest. The saguaro is king of the cacti and stands as high as 50 feet when full grown. Its arms, ranging from 12 to 24 feet, tower into the sky. Its average life-span is about 200 years. The root system extends outward 65 feet from the base, soaking up all the moisture resident in the desert soil during rain storms. Its elaborate system of pumps sends the water through the cactus. During a drought the saguaro can live up to four years without taking in more water because of its incredible storage system.

This is an illustration contrast. No couple has a saguaro marriage. We can't store up love, encouragement, affirmation, compliments, romantic experiences, times of intimate sharing and peak experiences. Even the best of marriages need to be jump-started from time to time. Commitments need to be renewed. Romance needs to be rekindled. Relationships need to be enriched.

Why do we celebrate anniversaries? Or go on a second honeymoon? Or attend a marriage enrichment weekend? Or renew wedding vows on silver and golden anniversaries? These are simply ways that we get a fresh start in marriage.

I once read that marriages may be made in heaven but the maintenance work takes place on earth. It's the maintenance work that makes or breaks a marriage. When you purchase a car, or an appliance or furniture the salesperson usually offers you a service contract. Why? Because he or she knows you'll need it! Everything requires upkeep — including marriage. So, let me ask you, What kind of service contract do you have for your marriage?

Here are some tips to help you jump-start your marriage if you're in a rut. Or, maybe if you just need to get a fresh start.

BACK TO THE FUTURE

Every couple needs occasionally to travel back in time to their wedding day. Picture the beautiful decorations, the lovely flowers and all the people who shared that joyous occasion with you. Most importantly, listen closely and hear the vows you spoke from your heart. What a powerful promise every couple makes:

> *I take you to be my wedded wife/husband, to have and to hold, from this day forward, for better, for worse, for richer, for poorer, in sickness and in health, to love and to cherish, till death us do part according to God's holy ordinance; and thereto, I pledge you my faith.*

These vows embody the real meaning of commitment. Commitment is a lost word in our contemporary vocabulary. People talk a lot about being happy, but very little about commitment. But there's no way to have a strong marriage that stands the test of time without a deep-settled commitment to the marriage covenant. The word commitment means to be dedicated to a cause, to be willing to make necessary sacrifices, to demonstrate ownership and to fulfill one's responsibilities.

The only way to stay married in an age of divorce is to learn the power of commitment. Every good marriage is deeply rooted in the soil of commitment. That's the secret to growing together through the seasons of life and weathering the storms that threaten every marriage.

People today seem to shy away from making commitments. They remind me of the story about the chicken and the pig. One morning the farmer came out to get some eggs for breakfast. When the chicken saw him coming toward the barn she brightened up and said to the pig, "Isn't it wonderful? We get to provide breakfast for the farmer and his family."

"That's easy for you to say," the pig replied. "All you have to do is make a contribution. I have to make a *total commitment!*"

Marriage takes more than an occasional contribution. Total commitment is required—till death us do part.

Let me tell you about a couple who jump-started their marriage in an almost miraculous way. They came to my office for marriage counseling. At least, he did. She put a damper on the session when she announced abruptly, "The only reason I agreed to come to counseling was to get my husband to understand that our marriage is over." She had been telling him for a couple of months that she was planning to divorce him. He hadn't taken her seriously. But she got through to him that day. No more discussion. No willingness to come for counseling. She left my office with her mind made up to get a divorce.

He called me a couple of days later and said, "I don't know what to do. My wife has taken all her things out of the house and is moving back home to North Carolina. She has an interview tomorrow for a new job."

Over the next few days he sank into deep depression. He called me and said, "I've given up on God." Later, when he got past his anger with God he started reading what the Bible says about marriage and, in particular, what it says about how a husband is suppose to treat his wife. He discovered that marriage is a covenant before God, not a contract. With new resolve, he determined to get his wife back. Personally, I thought he was setting himself up for a big disappointment. I've never seen anyone more set on a divorce and more fed up with a relationship than she was the day she sat in my office.

For the first two weeks after she left him, he called me non-stop. "I believe God can save my marriage," he would say. I would tell him, "God will help *you* save your marriage. God is not responsible for the shape your marriage is in. You and your wife are responsible." Tough words, but true. And he took them to heart.

After that I didn't hear from him for several weeks. I figured their relationship was over. Then I got the shock of my life. He approached me at church as I was leaving after a service. With a big smile on his face he proceeded to tell me that he and his wife had been seeing each other. He said their love was as fresh as it was when they dated in high school. Never had they experienced so much love for each other. Then he asked if I would see them again for counseling. I was flabbergasted.

Out of curiosity I met with them. During the first session I couldn't help but ask her, "What made the difference? Ten weeks ago you didn't want anything to do with your husband. You were determined to divorce him and get on your life. Now you're telling me that you are more in love than you've ever been."

She said, "After I left him, he began to show me more love and respect than I've ever known. He has treated me special; like I'm the most important person in the world to him. He has resurrected my love that I thought was dead forever."

Then she turned, looked directly at him said, "Please don't ever change."

Needless to say, they jump-started their marriage. Shortly after they got back together I had the privilege of leading them through the renewal of their marriage vows. Then they went on a second honeymoon. You may be wondering whether or not they made it. Well, I am glad to inform you that they are happily married. About a year later she got pregnant. Something, by the way, that had always terrified him. Today, they are the proud parents of a beautiful baby boy.

They got a fresh start. And so can you. It all boils down to commitment and the ability to renew your commitment when times get tough.

WATCH OUT FOR THE POTHOLES IN THE ROAD

We also need to look out for the potholes in the road. No matter how strong your marriage is, the road you travel is filled with potholes that can seriously damage any relationship. Keep your eyes open for...

Communication breakdown. Open, honest communication forms the heart and soul of a good marriage. Remember what we said earlier, communication is conversation with a purpose. Nothing destroys a relationship faster than the lack of communication. The loneliest people in the world are those trapped in a marriage where the communication lines have been cut. So open wide your heart and let your mate know the real you. Share your thoughts, your dreams, your aspirations, your fears. Hide nothing. Keep no secrets. And you'll discover the secret of real intimacy.

When conflict comes, and it will, resolve your differences quickly. As the Bible says, *"Don't let the sun go down while you are still angry."* When you do, you will be able to use conflict as a growth experience rather than allowing it to divide you.

Time together. Do you remember when you and your partner first met? How you would rearrange your schedule just so you could be together? Don't ever lose that sense of pursuit. What a tragedy when a couple takes each other for granted. So, keep the romance alive. The lack of time together spoils so many marriages. Unhappy couples usually have their time parceled out to everything and everyone else, instead of spending it together. Let's be honest: We all get caught up in the rat race.

The three greatest enemies we all face are the clock, the calendar and the telephone. They invade our lives with the tyranny of the urgent. C.S. Lewis remarked, "Hurry is not of the devil; it is the devil!" Americans are too busy — driven by an endless list of errands to run, meetings to attend, deadlines to make, committees to serve and tasks to fulfill. We carry beepers and cellular phones so that people can track us down at any hour of the day. By the time we've finished meeting all the demands of the urgent, we have little or no time left for the important.

The point is—guard your time together! Its like the story about a Kansas cyclone that hit a farmhouse one morning just before dawn. It lifted off the roof, picked up the bed on which a farmer and his wife were sleeping and set them down gently in the next county.

When the ordeal was over and the shock wore off, the farmer's wife burst into tears.

"It's okay, sweetheart. Don't be scared," her husband said, "We're not hurt."

"I'm not crying because I'm scared," she said between sobs, "I'm crying because I'm happy. This is the first time we've been out together in fourteen years!"

Ingratitude. Gratitude is the cure for the criticism, discontentment and unhappiness that destroys many marriages. Being thankful frees us from unrealistic demands, expectations and selfishness. Cicero, the Roman poet, noted, "A thankful heart is not only the greatest virtue, it is the parent of all virtues." Happy couples are thankful for each other. Unhappiness is often a symptom of an ungrateful heart.

But let's be honest, sometimes it's difficult to be thankful. We get on each other's nerves, have a fight or just get tired of each other's irritating idiosyncrasies. It's at times like these when we need to give thanks. One night the scholar Matthew Henry was robbed. Returning home, he wrote this prayer of thanksgiving in his journal:

I thank Thee first because I was never robbed before; second, because although they took my purse, they did not take my life; third, although they took my all, it was not much; and fourth, because it was I who was robbed and not I who robbed.

Count your blessings even when times are tough. Charles Boswell, former football star at the University of Alabama, held high hopes of a professional football career. Tragically, he lost his eye sight in combat during World War II. Later, however, he went on to become the National Blind Golf Champion 17 times. In an interview he was asked how he could have ever accomplished such a feat. He said, "I never count what I've lost. I only count what I have left." That's why every married couples needs to do to be happy.

Demands and expectations. Unrealistic demands and expectations suffocate a relationship. Covenant living means unconditional love. Not love *if.* Or, love *because of.* But love *in spite of.* Take your unrealistic demands and expectations, along with that secret wish-list for the perfect partner and rid your heart of them, once and for all. Here's a suggestion: Write all your unrealistic demands and expectations on a piece of paper and then burn it in a fireplace. As the flames consume the list, visualize them being destroyed freeing you to experience the joy of unconditional love for the one who is the most important person in the world to you.

Indifference. Justice Oliver Wendel Holmes once remarked, "Most people die with their music still in them." Sadly, this is true for many couples. They settle for so little when they could enjoy so much. What a tragedy to see a couple take their relationship for granted, neglect the garden of love and live indifferently toward each other.

Helen Keller made an interesting observation about human nature when she said, "Science may have found a cure for most evils; but it has found no remedy for the worst of them all — the apathy of human beings." The difference between mediocrity and greatness is diligence. The Bible says, *"Whatever you do (including marriage), work at it with all your heart, as working for the Lord not for men."*[1]

Pursue your partner as passionately and persistently as you did before you got married. Many couples lose their sense of diligence and let their marriage fly on autopilot. But it won't fly very long. Marriages left on autopilot crash and burn eventually.

I remember watching a television interview with Arnold Schwarzenegger conducted by Barbara Walters. He won the Mr. Universe title eight consecutive times and has gone on to a successful acting career. She asked him, "Do you have a philosophy of life?"

He replied with a big smile—"Stay hungry."

That's great advice for couples.

Well, I could go on and on listing potential potholes but I think you get the point. Misplaced priorities. Addictive behaviors. Interference from family members. Constant bickering. The list is endless. When you detect them confront them as quickly and aggressively as a surgeon operates on a cancer.

You may be wondering, Is it possible for any couple, regardless of the problems they face, to make a come-back and get a fresh start in their marriage?

AGAINST ALL ODDS

If you were an artist and decided to paint a picture to best portray the meaning of hope, what would you paint? Years ago an artist named Watts titled one of his paintings, "Hope." It portrayed a woman sitting on a world that had treated her most unfairly. Her eyes are bandaged, preventing her from seeing her way ahead. In her hands she holds a harp, all the strings except one are broken. Triumphantly she strikes that last string, and from it a beautiful melody lifts from the harp over her world and fills her dark night with stars.

In the midst of life's disappointments, God gives us a harp with a single string called hope. When we play it, we fill our hearts, our homes and our world with the triumphant spirit of hope that declares, *"With God all things are possible."*

Regardless of the difficulties, disappointments and failures a couple experience, there is hope. Every marriage possesses the innate ability to regenerate itself and to be "born again." Absolutely, no marriage is hopeless; that is, if both parties are willing to forgive, to recommit and to make the necessary changes to build a solid relationship together. But, I must add, it takes both of them to make it happen. The basic law of marriage is, *"Two become one."* If they do, with the help of God, all things are possible.

I'm sure you have known a married couple who experienced such serious problems that you doubted if there was any hope from them. Maybe you find yourself in that kind of troubled marriage right now. Let me assure you, there is hope. The greatest gift God gives us in this life is the gift of hope. Its true: *"With God all things are possible."* And that includes troubled marriages.

You can jump-start your marriage, no matter how much damage has been done; or how apathetic you may have become about the relationship; or how hopeless you are that things will never work out. You can renew your covenant, start over and experience a brand new season of marital joy.

Here's a letter I received from a couple who found hope and jump-started their marriage before it was too late:

Dear Dr. Cooper:

My wife and I are the couple you remarried in your office a couple of years ago. To start, I'd best describe our early experiences so you can better see how God so wonderfully used them.

We were both raised in religious environments, although I received a much stronger dose of a "works mentality." We met and were married in college. Neither of us understood the true meaning and purpose of marriage although we both felt we were good people, especially by comparative standards. We both entered the marriage fully expecting to be good, but gradually the battle of wills created a communication vacuum that eventually led to divorce.

My wife became so stifled and unappreciative that she turned to a career for relief. This further complicated matters. As I received less and less attention, I got even more overbearing. Her career led her into a relationship with her boss and both of them became involved in a humanistic movement.

Being the "driven to do good" person I was, I began trying to figure out how I was going to save her from the evils of this group and save our marriage and family. The most amazing thing happened, as I was trying so hard to save her, God saved me! Somehow, in spite of my individual efforts, God put Christian people, and circumstances in my life that turned me to Christ.

The changes in me were enough for her to start seeing in me something she'd rarely seen; something worth getting back to. At the same time God was working in her heart.

The message I feel compelled to share is this...we let the power of God make the changes. My own efforts were always charged with emotion, usually self-serving, and predicated on an expected outcome. In spite of these efforts, our reconciliation came about as a result of God giving us His wisdom, and then putting the truth in our hearts to mesh it together like it was designed to be from the start...like it never could have been without the miserable circumstances that brought us to the end of our own efforts and into His.

And as He has promised, He continues to make everything work for our good. He has used our experience to show us how misguided we were, yet blessed. Without the divorce, God would not be the center of our commitment. Certainly, the pleasures of marriage have never been so special as they are now. Without a legalistic upbringing, the liberty of His word would not be so appreciated. Without the empty ritualism of our past, the freedom, joy and peace of Christ would not seem quite the blessing.

My prayer was simply that God would bring our family back together. He decided otherwise. His plan was to bring it back together in the full power and purpose for which He was originally intended.

AN OUNCE OF PREVENTION

As wonderful as their story is, its better to keep a marriage from ever getting to the place where a miracle is needed. As the adage goes, "An ounce of prevention is worth a pound of cure." And the best way to prevent marital disaster and to secure marital joy is to establish your marriage as a covenant before God, based on unconditional love, "till death us do part."

That's why it is so important to learn the difference between a covenant and a contract. So, let's take a minute and review what we've learned:

A Contract...	The Covenant...
is a two-party agreement	is based on an equal contribution
is based on an equal contribution	is based on mutuality
is conditional on the terms being met	is unconditional of the other's response
consists of demands and expectations	is based on sacrifice
is concerned with rights being met	is willing to surrender one's rights
often has power struggles	is characterized by mutual submission
demands full payment of debts	forgives all debts

The only thing that remains is for you to decide which way you will go. Will you choose the path of the contract, trying to strike the perfect agreement, driven to have all of your expectations fulfilled and your demands met? Or, will you choose the ancient path of the covenant, learning and growing through the ups and downs of married life, sustained by the power of unconditional love? The Old Testament prophet put it well: *"Stand at the crossroads and look; ask for the ancient paths, as where the good way is, and walk in it, and you will find rest for your souls."*

I am confident you will choose correctly.

PUT IT IN WRITING

If you're like me, writing down your commitments is beneficial. So let me encourage you to put your covenant in writing. Then share it with your partner. You'll be amazed at the impact it makes.

Several years ago I was encouraged to do this. I found it tremendously helpful to give my marriage covenant some serious thought. I want to leave it with you.

A MARRIAGE COVENANT

You and I have a treasured relationship which I view as a gift from God. As a special gift of God to me, I will accept you in your uniqueness; respect you in your differences from me; allow you room for individual expression; seek to understand and meet your needs; refrain from being overbearing and demanding; grant you the freedom to fail; forgive you for your errors; restore you when you stumble; bear your burdens when you cannot carry them alone; give thanks daily for you and pray for you; provide for your needs within my means; encourage the realization of your full potential; remind you often through word and deed that you are the most important person in the world to me.

When we enter troubled waters, I will seek to understand and listen to your feelings; openly express my own feelings; strive to express my anger appropriately; endeavor to work together with you as a team against our adversities and never to oppose you; refrain from threats which undermine your security in me; fulfill my commitment to become one flesh by the grace of God till death do us part.

As your husband, I pledge myself to love you as Christ loves the church; to give myself up for you; to share the responsibilities and rewards of our home as an equal partner; to be considerate of you and to treat you with respect; to communicate my love openly, freely, and frequently; to support you in your personal goals and aspirations; to give you the freedom to become the fullness of all that God created you to be; and to be faithful in all the privileges and responsibilities of being your husband.

DON'T FORGET THE KING

I have thought long and hard about how to end this book. And I have decided to end it with a story that underscores the most important key to being happily married.

An art gallery in Germany features a painting that is not quite finished. King Frederick the Great is artistically portrayed as talking to his generals. In the center of the painting is a section etched in a charcoal outline, indicating the artist's intention to paint a person. But the artist died before the painting was finished. He had painted the background and the generals first, but the king he left till last. He died before painting the king. Today his work of art stands as the contribution of a man who omitted the king.

Don't forget to paint the king, Jesus Christ, in the portrait of your marriage, and you will experience the joys of covenant love, *"for better <u>not</u> worse."*

REFERENCES

INTRODUCTION

1   Jeanette Lauer and Robert Lauer, "Marriages Made To Last," *Psychology Today* (June, 1985), 22-26.
2   *Psychology Today*, (March/April, 1996), 11.

CHAPTER ONE: Seven Myths Of Marriage

1   Karen Peterson, "Single Life Gaining On Couplehood," *USA Today* (March 13, 1996).
2   See Gen 2:24.
3   Derric Johnson, *Lists, The Book* (Orlando: Y.E.S.S. Press, 1993), 51.
4   Francine Klagsbrun, *Married People: Staying Together in the Age of Divorce* (New York: Bantam Books, 1985).
5   David Blankenhorn, *Fatherless America* (New York: Basic Books, 1995), 76.
6   Willard F. Harley, *His Needs, Her Needs* (Grand Rapids: Fleming H. Revell a division of Baker Book House Company, copyright 1986, 1994).
7   See Phil 4:13, 19.
8   See 1 Thess 5:18.
9   See Ruth 1:16, 17.
10 Max Lucado, *On The Anvil* (Used by permission of Tyndale House Publishers, Inc. All Rights Reserved, (c) 1985), 143-144.

CHAPTER TWO: Covenant Versus Contract

1   William J. Bennett, *The Index of Leading Cultural Indicators* (New York: Simon & Schuster, 1994), 57.
2   Associated Press release,"Tennessee considering 'covenant marriage' legislation" (*The Atlanta/Journal Constitution*), October, 10, 1997.
3   See Isa 50:1; 54:4-6; Isa 62:4,5; Jer 2:2; Ezek 16; Hos 2:16-20.
4   See Rev 21:2.
5   See Eph 5:31.
6   Walter A. Elwell, *Evangelical Dictionary of Theology* (Grand Rapids: Baker Book House, 1984), 276.

7   *The Interpreter's Dictionary of The Bible*, s.v., "Covenant" by G.E. Mendenhall (New York: Abingdon, 1962). Used by permission.

8   Arnold B. Rhodes, *The Mighty Acts of God* (Richmond: The CLC Press, 1964), 82.

9   Taken from *New International Dictionary of New Testament Theology*, edited by Collin Brown. (Copyright (c) 1975 by The Zondervan Corporation. Used by permission of Zondervan Publishing House.), 368 (parenthesis added).

10 Paul Wells, "Covenant, Humanity, and Scripture," *Westminster Theological Journal*, Vol. 48, No. 1 (Spring, 1986), 25.

11 See Jn 1:12.

12 See Deut 6:6-8; Jer 31:31-34.

13 Vines, Unger, and White, eds., *Vines Expository Dictionary of Biblical Words* (Nashville: Used by permission of Thomas Nelson, Inc.,1985), 142.

14 Merwyn Johnson, *Locke On Freedom* (Austin: Best Printing Co., 1978), 54.

15 Ibid., 54.

16 See Lk 6:27-38.

17 See 2 Tim 2:13.

18 Walther Eichrodt, *Theology of the Old Testament* Vol. 1 (Pennsylvania: The Westminster Press, 1961), 54.

19 See Rom 8:31,35-39, Phillips Translation.

20 See Hos 14:4.

CHAPTER THREE: WHO'S IN CHARGE?

1   Cited in *The Best of Bits and Pieces*, Arthur F. Lenehan, ed., (Fairfield, NJ: The Economics Press: 1994), 196. Phone 800-526-2554

2   See Gal 3:28.

3   Quoted by F.W. Boreham in, "An Epic of Concentration," *A Late Lark Singing* (London: Epworth Press, 1945), 128.

4   James Harrison Hunter, *Culture Wars* (Basic Books, 1991), 177.

5   Those who hold to this position base their views on such New Testament passages as 1 Corinthians 11:3, Ephesians 5:22-24, Colossians 3:18, Titus 2:4,5, and 1 Peter 3:1-6 where Christian wives are admonished to "be submissive to your husbands" (1 Pt 3:1). The call to submission even applies to wives who are married to unbelieving husbands in an effort to win them to Christ (1 Pet 3:1,2).

6   Karl Barth, *Church Dogmatics*, Vol. 3, No. 4 (Edinburgh: T & T Clark, 1958), 165-183.

7   See Mk 10:45; Jn 13:1-12; Phil 2:5-8.

8   See Matt 28:18; Lk 10:19.

9   See Rev 3:21.

10   See Eph 5:21.

11   *The Expositor's Bible Commentary,* Vol. 11 edited by Frank E. Gaebelein. (Copyright (c) 1978 by The Zondervan Corporation. Used by permission of Zondervan Publishing House), 75.

12   See Titus 2:4; Eph 5:33.

13   See 1 Pt 3:7.

14   Paul E. Steele, "Marriage and the Family," *Applying the Scriptures*, ed. Kenneth S. Kantzer (Grand Rapids: Academic Books, 1987), 204- 205.

15   Ibid., 205.

16   See 1 Pt 2:9; Rev 1:5,6.

17   See Mark 10:35-45.

18   See Eph 5:25.

19   Roy McCloughry, *The Eye of the Needle* (Inter-Varsity Press, England, 1990), 31-38.

CHAPTER FOUR: CARING ENOUGH TO COMMUNICATE

1   See Prov 12:18; 15:1; 18:12; 21:23.

2   See Eph 4:29.

3   Robert Fisher, *Quick To Listen, Slow To Speak* (Used by permission of Tyndale House Publishers, Inc. All Rights Reserved., (c) 1987 Pathway Press, Cleveland, Tennessee)

4   James F. Lynch, *The Language of the Heart: The Body's Response to Human Dialogue* (New York: Basic Books, 1985).

5   See Prov 18:13.

6   Robert C. Crosby and Pamela Crosby, "Now That's A Good Question," *Focus On The Family* (December, 1996).

7   Becky Freeman, "Listen Up!," *Virtue* (May/June, 1997), 46-48.

8   Cited by Becky Freeman in "Listen Up!," *Virtue* (May/June, 1997), 46-48.

9   Cited in *The Best of Bits And Pieces*, Arthur F. Lenehan, ed., (Fairfield, NJ: The Economics Press: 1994), 65-66. Phone 800-526-2554

CHAPTER FIVE: MAKING THE MOST OF YOUR MONEY

1   See Ecc 10:19.

2   See Lk 6:38; Acts 20:35.

3   John Haggai, *Paul J. Meyer and the Art of Giving* (Atlanta: Kobrey Press, 1994), 19-20.

4   Joseph McAuliffe, "What To Teach About Money," *Ministries Today* (March/April, 1988), 61.

5   Olivia Mellan, *Overcoming Overspending* (New York: Walker and Co., 1995), 24-25.

6   *The Kiplinger Washington Letter* (Reproduced by Kiplinger Washington Editors, Inc.) May 30, 1997.

7   Cited in *Money* (April, 1987).

8   Adapted from the material of Thomas J. Stanley, "Why You're Not As Wealthy As You Should Be" in *Medical Economics*, (July 20, 1992).

9   *The Kiplinger Washington Letter* (Reproduced by Kiplinger Washington Editors, Inc.) January 3, 1997.

10   Adapted from Henry Edward Felder, *Making Ends Meet: Financial Planning for the Christian Family* (Hagerstown: Review & Herald Publishing, 1994).

11   Elizabeth Razzi, "How Smart Couples Handle Their Money," (Kiplinger Personal Finance Magazine, June 1996).

CHAPTER SIX: Loving Your Way To Better Sex

1   Gary R. Collins, *Christian Counseling: A Comprehensive Guide,* (USA: Word, 1980), 300.

2   See Prov 5:18, 19; SS 8:6-7.

3   F. Philip Rice, *Sexual Problems In Marriage* (Philadelphia: The Westminster Press, 1978), 17.

4   Andrew M. Greenly, *Sexual Intimacy* (Chicago: Thomas Moore Assn., 1973).

5   Leo Buscaglia, *Loving Each Other* (New York: Fawcett Columbine, 1984), 69-70.

6   Rice, 15, 16.

7   Richard Restak, *The Brain: The Last Frontier* (Garden City, N.Y.: Doubleday and Company, 1979), 197.

8   Ibid., 206.

9   Dr. James Dobson, *What Wives Wish Their Husbands Knew About Women* (Wheaton, IL: Used by permission of Tyndale House Publishers, Inc., All Rights Reserved (c) 1975), 117.

10   James Lincoln Collier, "It Is Different For Women" (*Reader's Digest,* January, 1982), 84-87.

11   Ibid., 85.

12   Ibid., 86.

13   Kathleen McCoy, "5 Sex Secrets Women Wish Husbands Knew" (*Reader's Digest,* January, 1988), 91-94.

14   Kathleen McCoy, "Five Sex Secrets Men Wish Wives Knew" (*Redbook*, October, 1985).

15   Taken from *Sexual Happiness In Marriage* by Herbert J. Miles. (Copyright (c) 1967 by Zondervan Publishing House. Used by permission of Zondervan Publishing House.), 158.

16   Daniel J. Dolesh and Sherelynn Lehman, *Love Me, Love Me Not* (New York: McGraw Hill, 1985).

CHAPTER SEVEN: THE MISSING LINK

1   James Dobson, "Dr. Dobson's Prescription for a Successful Marriage" *Focus On The Family* (October, 1987), 2.
2   Ibid., 61.
3   See Ecc 4:12.
4   See Rom 5:5.
5   Dietrich Bonhoeffer, quoted in Larry Christensen, *The Christian Family* (Minneapolis: Bethany Fellowship, 1970), 9.
6   See Phil 1:6.
7   David Benner, *Psychotherapy and the Spiritual Quest* (Grand Rapids: Baker, 1988), 104.
8   Augustine, *Basic Writings of Saint Augustine,* Ed. and trans. W. Oates, Vol. 1 (Grand Rapids: Baker, 1980), 3.
9   See Gen 5:24; 2 Chr 20:7; Ex 33:11; 1 Sam 13:14; Jn 15:15.
10 Frank Pittman, *Private Lies: Infidelity and the Betrayal of Intimacy* (New York: W.W. Norton, 1990).
11 Catherine Houck, "What Makes A Marriage Last," *Reader's Digest* (March, 1996), 71-72.
12 Reprinted with permission of Simon & Schuster from *The People's Religion by* George Gallup, Jr. and Jim Castelli, 64.
13 Chuck Colson, "Can We Be Good Without God?" *Crosswinds,* Vol. 2, No. 2 (1994), 32.
14 See Deut 6:6,7.
15 George Barna, *Moody Magazine,* (June, 1994), 12.
16 See Gen 2:25.
17 Albert Ellis and Robert A. Harper, *A New Guide to Rational Living* (Hollywood: Melvin Publishers, 1975).
18 C. Austin Miles, "In the Garden" (Rodeheaver Co., 1940).
19 Kenneth L. Woodward, "Is God Listening?" *Newsweek* (March 31, 1997).

CHAPTER EIGHT: TWENTY-FOUR HOUR FORGIVENESS

1   See Matt 6:14, 15; Mk 11:25; Matt 7:1,2; Heb 12:15.
2   *The Anna Russell Song Book* (Secaucus: Citadel Press).
3   See Rom 14:23; Jas 4:17; 1Jn 3:4; 5:17.
4   See Matt 18:23-35.
5   See 2 Cor 5:18, 19.
6   See Matt 5:23, 24.
7   See Rom 12:19.

8   See Deut 24:1-4.

9   See Luke 15:20-24.

10   See Rom 12:21.

11   See Lk 6:27, 28.

12   E. Stanley Jones, *The Way* (Garden City: Doubleday, 1978), 124-130.

CHAPTER NINE: JUMP-STARTING YOUR MARRIAGE

1   See Col 3:23 (parenthesis added).